Nomadic Moonlight

A Decade of Full Moons Living on the Go

KENNY FLANNERY

Contact: HoboLifestyle@gmail.com

Editing by: Julie Butler

ISBN: 979-8-38-784528-4

BEFORE THE MOONS

Freedom can be hard to recognize. Many of us keep walls around ourselves, ceilings between us and the moon, and attach ourselves to relationships, careers and philosophies that further box us in.

Plenty of people thrive within this structure. Plenty more, however, don't. Life is a canvas with unique possibilities and we work with what we've got. I turned mine into a hitchhiking sign.

In the summer of 2007, I began living out of a backpack, embracing an untethered lifestyle of spontaneity. Travel is a natural component and so I'm often walking, hitchhiking, road-tripping, or flying out to the next destination, be it new frontiers or familiar stomping grounds.

Free of frivolous obligations, free of unaligned responsibilities and free to seize opportunity. Hitchhiking in particular became a gateway into different perspectives and a proverbial "Schrödinger's Cat" of possibilities.

I cut ties with an apartment and steady jobs but have maintained many of my relationships with friends and family. My goal was not to go into the wild of the world seeking separation, but rather to explore how far my freedom could take me by hopping on the most enticing streams available.

Here, we'll take the journey of my first decade on the road through glimpses, checking in on every full moon to see how I was moving along. I'll answer common questions, like how I've afforded to stay on the go, where I sleep while traveling, how romance is possible on the go, and why beer is so damn powerful.

It was interesting putting this together and seeing just how many important events lined up with full moons, whether it was meeting lifelong friends, finding love, or even sitting in a jail cell... twice. Freedom, right?

Some back-to-back full moons seemed misleading, appearing in the same location even though I'd traveled hundreds if not thousands of miles in between, only to end up back in the same place for the next one.

I honestly don't know how much of a direct effect the moon has on individuals as it pushes and pulls the tides, but there seems to be something to it.

I can't help but hint at some of the adventures in between, but we'll stick to the moonlight as much as possible.

Adventures were had, relationships rose, some set, and with experience came a slicker ride when I stayed in the flow. So, starting with the first full moon of freedom, we'll check in moon-by-moon over the first decade of my rambling around the planet and end in the perfect place to celebrate.

TYPES OF MOONS

First, a quick explanation of the special types of full moons that I've noted along the journey.

A **Super Full Moon** occurs when the moon is in its closest orbit to earth, looking bigger and brighter. A **Micro Full Moon** is the opposite.

A **Total Lunar Eclipse** occurs when the sun is behind the earth, casting a shadow on the moon. A **Partial Lunar Eclipse** is — you guessed it — when there's only a partial shadow. Finally, a **Penumbral Lunar Eclipse** is when there's only a subtle shadow.

A **Blue Moon** is not a blue-colored moon but is how we refer to the third full moon in a season with four full moons or the second full moon in a calendar month.

Full Mooning is what I did to that bouncer in Newport Beach.

For those of you reading this digitally, most entries include a link (click the location text) to blog posts or videos related to that story — just in case you want to know more about a particular adventure or what happened in-between moons.

You can also go directly to HoboLifestyle.com, which is the hub of all my stories, videos, pictures and a podcast.

Alright, let's hit the road.

JUNE 30, 2007

New York City

This was the final day of June in 2007 — the last month in which I paid rent anywhere.

I was done with a soul-eroding job that made me just enough money to live nearby and keep coming to work. An unfulfilling cycle of redundancy to the level of a dress code requiring us to wear the same red tie on Monday, the blue one on Tuesday, the yellow one... you get it.

All that is over now. I'd given away everything I couldn't carry on my shoulders and started making moves.

I don't recall seeing the full moon peeking through New York's forest of buildings that night, but it was calling for me. I had one last hurrah with my roommates, Mark and Sean, who were brothers and my friends from childhood.

Even after traveling around the world, I still hold New York in the highest regard. It's a breeding ground of possibility in its own right and, for me, a hub of many familiar faces.

I'd walk those streets under many full moons to come, but now, it's westbound to break myself into this new way of life.

JULY 29, 2007

Jackson Hole, Wyoming

The girl I'd left in New York was easing the transition by my side at this moment in Wyoming. I'd hitched a ride on a family road trip to get out here, and she'd flown out for a week to be with me.

She'd be flying back to New York and my family would be driving back east as well, but this was a one-way trip to everywhere for me.

We'd spent the day at the lake and hiked around the mountain, now lounging for the night in comfort. This wasn't lost on me; I was taking it all in, knowing that soon my days would become unpredictable. I knew there'd be nights camping, that showers wouldn't always be a given and meals would be random.

My giant backpack was bursting at the seams and what I couldn't fit inside was strapped on the outside. I even had a couple of smaller bags to fit the extra nonsense I thought I needed. I was a walking yard sale for now, but I'd soon learn the value of purging it all. At this moment, it was a symbol of freedom.

A transitional moon, of sorts, in one of the most beautiful places in the country that would attract me again and again, that's for sure. Soak it in, but keep it moving.

AUGUST 28, 2007

Sacramento, California (Total Lunar Eclipse)

In my senior year of high school, I channeled Chris Farley when explaining my passion to "live in a van, down by the river!" rather than pursue college of any sort.

I had a passion for audio engineering and this was leveraged against me. I was convinced to get an associate's (and then a bachelor's) degree at a school near Orlando, Florida.

Why is this relevant to this full moon? This school is where I became friends with Aaron. He claims to be the first person to pick me up "hitchhiking" when offering me a ride from school to our apartment complex on a rainy day.

After hearing of my new "hobo" ambitions, he paid for my train ticket to Portland (after parting with family in Montana) and then a plane ticket to his place in California.

"Hobo 2.0 Lifestyle" is how I was framing my foray into the world. Downtime days like this one I spent on my laptop, either working on a travel site I'd created, my travel blog, or my travel videos.

SEPTEMBER 26, 2007

San Diego, California

Wandering the San Diego streets, I admire the bright orange moon in the darkening sky, pondering where I'll stay for the night. I pass up some decent stealth camping spots because even though it's dark, it's still relatively early. In the end, I lucked out with a last-minute Couchsurfing host.

"Couchsurfing" was the first wildly popular hospitality site. Back then it was free, with a network of friendly people around the world willing to host travelers in their homes for a few nights.

It fell into my "Hobo 2.0" concept, and I first had success with it during my week in Portland in between the train and plane ride, then again in Los Angeles a week before now.

I walked for a few hours this night, knowing I'd be meeting up with Aaron the next day when he flew down to see his girlfriend, who was going to school in San Diego. It wasn't until around 10 p.m. that I got a call from someone on the Couchsurfing site, willing to host me on their futon at the last minute.

The Couchsurfing site — and others like Trustroots, BeWelcome, and eventually Couchers — would be deeply intertwined into my rambling lifestyle over the years to come.

OCTOBER 25, 2007

Oklahoma City to Las Vegas (Super Full Moon)

Greyhound has got to be the sketchiest way to travel in the United States and I was on the moonlit bus to Las Vegas, adding yet another story to its checkered reputation.

I'd completed my first big hitchhiking trip from California to Oklahoma City, and I probably should have hitchhiked back, but I still had a little money and had gotten a taste for Vegas earlier in the month, so I was eager to get back.

The guy sitting next to me, Jason, scammed me out of $200. Not right away, but instead we became friendly, and once in Vegas, he joined me in a multi-day rager with some of Aaron's friends I'd met in San Diego who were also in Vegas.

The day came when he had a bulky story about a wire transfer and his mom and this and that — I was suspicious, but also naive enough to fall for it. He'd watched me win several hundred dollars playing craps and decided he wanted it more than I did.

More on Vegas later — the debauchery would escalate.

NOVEMBER 24, 2007

Ijamsville, Maryland (Super Full Moon)

I gravitated east for the first time since taking off, landing at my uncle and aunt's place for Thanksgiving. My family was happy to see me still alive, perhaps as alive as I'd ever been.

Since Vegas, I've had even more Greyhound and hitchhiking stories stacking up, from California to South Carolina and everywhere in between. I was addicted.

With Christmas a month away, I decided I'd pay a little visit to New York City again and see what the air felt like in my new skin. I also figured I'd bounce around to Philly and all the other spots nearby that I'd mostly ignored when I lived so close.

I've noticed it often, especially since I started traveling, that people often ignore the treasures in their own backyard, perhaps assuming they're "right there" and "of course" they'll check them out one day, maybe by accident.

It became a common theme, hearing lines like "you know more about my country than I do," or even discovering amazing little bars or parks a few blocks from someone's house that just wasn't on their routine path. It took a traveler to show them their own local gems.

DECEMBER 23, 2007

A Chinatown jail cell, New York City

My first time visiting friends back in the Northeast since starting my life on the road, and here we go — at the exact moment the moon was at its fullest, I'm in a holding cell in Chinatown.

A group of us took the subway from Queens to Grand Central to catch a Connecticut-bound train for a family Christmas party. Moments after passing through the turnstile, I felt a tug at my leg and was spun around by two police officers.

They pulled a folding knife from my jeans pocket, and while they couldn't decide if it was "too big" or "opened too quickly," they stubbornly decided they had to book me for it.

I stood handcuffed, waiting for additional officers to take me away as the whirlwind of Grand Central commuters whizzed by. The last girl I'd been with before leaving the city was with me and she couldn't help but initiate a makeout session to make the scene all the more ridiculous — the cops shut that down when they noticed it, real quick.

I was in the holding cell for less than a couple of hours with paperwork and fingerprints and the rest of it. That should have been the end of it, but it would end up dragging me back to New York for more moons than necessary.

JANUARY 22, 2008

Astoria, Queens (New York City)

Between moons, I'd been as far west as Las Vegas (a growing habit), but now back again to New York to deal with the court date for the knife.

On this night, however, I officially launched my travel site. I'd later call it "Trip Hopping," which was initially a catch-all transportation search engine. At first, being a bit of a self-taught coder nerd, I'd built it just for myself. It searched for buses, trains and flights; driving directions and gas prices; Craigslist rideshare posts; and even a database of hitchhiking spots. Basically, it uncovered every possible way to get from point A to point B.

It was a bit of an obsession, as you'll see it pop up on some future moons and then fade into the darkness.

My court date was just two days away. For such a silly thing, it sure did get dragged out.

FEBRUARY 20, 2008

Phoenix, Arizona (Total Lunar Eclipse)

Despite my court date resulting in just another court date — an obnoxious month later in NYC — I'd found a ride across the country to Arizona on Craigslist (thanks, Trip Hopping) from someone who just wanted help driving and not a dollar at all for gas.

On this particular day, before the moon reached its absolute fullest point in the evening, I hitchhiked up from Tucson to Phoenix where I met Larry. I'd found him on the Couchsurfing site, and unbeknownst to either of us then, we'd become lifelong friends.

He was a prolific host when it came to Couchsurfing, not only hosting hundreds of people over the years but also organizing meetups that ranged from nights out at the bar to camping trips involving waterfalls and helicopters.

We vibed immediately, particularly when it came to the travel site I'd started. In fact, the name "Trip Hopping" emerged in his kitchen while we got further hyped on building it up.

Another full moon, another epic introduction. Maybe there is something to it.

MARCH 21, 2008

New York City

My court date was a week away, pulling me back to New York yet again. Since Arizona, I'd hitchhiked to Oklahoma and taken a spontaneous road trip to Denver where I pretended to be a traveling musician's manager, among other hijinks. But I had to zig-zag my way back to New York for some silly knife nonsense.

On this day, I joined my old friends, Mark and Sean, as they got written up for playing music in the subway station. Perhaps it was mystical solidarity. Court dates for everyone, woo-hoo!

The edges of freedom are fuzzy. I started by saying that we work with what we've got, as it can be quite different for each of us.

Outside of thought, there is no ultimate freedom, no "pure" or "true" freedom to be had. Physics and societal pressure present plenty of limits and consequences. You're not free to leap over a building with nothing but your basketball sneakers and in the USA, if you kill somebody or play music in the subway station without a permit, you may just get a ticket, be handcuffed, or be forced into a cage.

And that's fine. It may just be that everything you desire to say and do is well within the limits. So when I think of "being free," I think of using all the space between. Not creating false barriers and not restraining myself with "popular" ideals that don't fit my own.

APRIL 20, 2008

Philadelphia, Pennsylvania

Philly is a hell of a city, and this was another good trek through. I spent this night with a girl from high school at a dive bar, throwing down cheap beers and catching up back at her place.

The result of my court date was a mandatory three days of community service. And if that was it, fine, but it also meant I needed to come back to court — again — to show proof I'd done that community service.

If not for all the friends and impromptu adventures I was having in the northeast, I would have felt more of a drag from this, but I was getting by just fine.

The next court date was nearly two moons away. Plenty of time to blast off into the west again.

MAY 19, 2008

San Diego, California (Blue Moon, Micro Full Moon)

Arrogant Bastard is a big beer from Stone Brewery, a classic, and there was at least one big bottle of it on the party bus. Aaron was getting married and tonight was the joint bachelor/bachelorette party wheeling around San Diego.

I could tell you about hitchhiking in an 18-wheeler for three days across the country, delivering cars in Denver, epic hospitality, Vegas antics, or stripping down with girls on the beaches of the Pacific Ocean, but those second-rate stories weren't even lit by the moon. Trash.

Instead, there's craft beer in the full moonlight, with a loveable bunch of drunken maniacs. Arrogant Bastard, in particular, is one of the beers that "leveled me up" in my growing obsession with craft beer.

OK, a quick Denver anecdote — my Couchsurfing host's roommate was homebrewing beer in the kitchen, which I had never seen before, and this too attributed to my interest.

You'll see much more about beer as we go on, and it'll stoke my travels a lot more than just a buzz here and there. Here on the party bus, though, buzz buzz.

JUNE 18, 2008

Philadelphia to New York City

With the moon at its fullest, I was again in Chinatown, but luckily not in a jail cell this time. My last court date had been a couple of days earlier and all I did was turn in some papers. It was a seemingly trivial thing to have hitchhiked across the country for, but at least that saga was over.

I'd fooled around in Philly again and hopped the bus to New York, my mind looking further to Boston. Beyond that, I'd just gotten word from Couchsurfing (the creators) that I was invited to volunteer with them up in Alaska where they were having a "collective."

At the time, they had no headquarters. Instead, they'd temporarily rent a house somewhere on the planet (like Thailand, Montreal and now Alaska) where a core group and volunteers would maintain the website for a few months at a time.

I'd couchsurfed with dozens of people already and loved the site, so when I saw they were looking for help, I offered. After reviewing my coding skills and obvious interest in tech and travel (and seeing a picture of me holding a duck they liked), they invited me to join them in Homer, Alaska.

This Chinatown bus was heading to New York, but my mind was drifting up through Canada, eager for the epic trek.

JULY 18, 2008

Pulaski, Tennessee

The moon shined on our tent for yet another night, pitched behind a motel only a couple of days shy of New Orleans. Is that on the way to Alaska coming from New York? Well, it was, so it is.

Heather had seen my post on Craigslist rideshare; I was looking for anyone driving out of the city to kickstart my long hitch to Alaska. She was a student at Tulane who'd come to Connecticut with a friend for a wedding; they were going to hitchhike back to Louisiana together until her friend broke her leg.

So, rather than offering me a ride, she messaged me and asked if I'd hitchhike with her. Not exactly the direct route, but it was... west at least? It was the right move.

We hitchhiked together through Cape Cod (again, wrong direction, right away), through upstate New York, kissed under a waterfall in West Virginia, volunteered at a music festival, ground-scored mushrooms (which I'd eat for the first time once getting to New Orleans) and set an unbelievable precedent for hitchhiking with a partner.

Inside the tent, with tall cans of cheap gas station beer, Heather started getting me hyped on New Orleans, which was finally within reach. I'd never been, but after this trip, I'd be sure to make it a regular stop.

AUGUST 16, 2008

Homer, Alaska (Penumbral Lunar Eclipse)

We took a boat across the bay on an "excursion," then back to the Couchsurfing house perched high above Homer with an ever-changing view of the water and clouds that gave texture to the sun's rays.

I'd been in Alaska for close to two weeks by this point, which is about how long it had taken to hitch up there from New Orleans and through Canada. They almost didn't let me across the border — apparently, they found my net worth of $40 to be unimpressive. But I finagled my way in.

Besides the odd excursion or pop-up party, two dozen of us in the house spent the days sitting at laptops, working on the Couchsurfing site in some capacity. I was making friends that I'd keep for a lifetime, including Mandie (from Australia) and Walter (from the Netherlands), with whom I'd form an epic hitchhiking trio, adventuring down to Vancouver after the collective.

It had now been just over a year since I'd hit the road myself, and I was dialed in. I'd gone through all the seasons, discovered hitchhiking, embraced Couchsurfing, and gone coast-to-coast numerous times, as far south as Mexico and now as north as Alaska. I'd run out of money, made money (more on that later), been stuck, found and kept coming out on top. And this was just the beginning.

SEPTEMBER 15, 2008

Seattle, Washington

Sex in the moonlight — there's a winner.

I'd hit it off with a red-headed wonder up in Vancouver a week earlier. When I told her I was hitchhiking to San Francisco next, she said she wanted to come and her roommate Rudy decided he'd join us as well.

Hitchhiking as a trio has its challenges, but I learned some tricks with Walter and Mandie. If cars weren't stopping, one of us would stay with the girl while the other would walk ahead. We'd either rendezvous down the road or wind up in the same car anyway.

After crossing the border into the U.S., I took the first solo turn. Walking further down the road, the sky darkened and the odds of getting a ride decreased. I admired the moon beaming down on me, but my trance was broken when a car pulled over.

Rudy and Kimmie had gotten a ride, and it took no convincing to have the driver scoop me up too. It was a great sight, seeing their faces as I got to the car. We got dropped just north of Seattle where we easily found a forest to camp in for the night. Kimmie and I slipped away from Rudy in the tent and found a suitable fallen tree to do the deed on.

Next time you're driving down the highway, just know there's a chance that right past the treeline there may just be a hobo and a beautiful vixen having the time of their lives.

OCTOBER 14, 2008

Willow Creek, California

My Canadian travel companions were well aware of something I had not been — the seasonal marijuana harvest in California. It was one of the reasons they'd joined me.

We'd had a hell of an adventure, slept in strange places and met a whole lot of people. Despite this, we hadn't scored any harvest work by the time we reached San Francisco. A gigolo named Starchild we met in Golden Gate Park put us up in his apartment and I bounced over to Berkeley to consider working full-time for Couchsurfing. Without the work, though, my latest travel clan had to fly back to Vancouver.

Days later, I was in Sacramento at Aaron's wedding when I got a phone call from someone we'd met on the trip — that's what landed me in Humboldt for this full moon.

"Trimming" is the gig many get for the pot harvest, cutting buds off branches and shaping them up, the final step before they reach the bag. Hours a day, often *all* day, clipping away. That's what I was now up to.

Before this, I'd made money through random one-off odd jobs, like helping my buddy Larry install glass doors at a building in Phoenix. This, however, would fund my traveling lifestyle for years to come, whenever I felt like dropping in for a harvest.

NOVEMBER 12, 2008

Las Vegas, Nevada

This was my sixth time in Las Vegas already. I was on my own this night in a comped Treasure Island hotel room. I'd hitched in from Berkeley with Mandie and another defecting Couchsurfing volunteer, but by now they'd flown on to the next thing.

Oh, Vegas. Back when I was in school in Orlando, I'd played a lot of poker, so the gambling leap to craps wasn't a big one. The first time I came to Vegas, a year earlier, I'd rolled the dice until the sun came up when my pockets were stuffed with more cash than I'd ever had.

I learned how to get comps, not only for free rooms but also buffets and even shows. Vegas became a go-to spot to either catch some rest, party with friends or go on craps binges with whatever cash I had, for better or worse. That town would only get wilder as the months and years stretched down the road.

Berkeley and the prospect of working for Couchsurfing were in my rearview. Mandie, and several others who'd been working for them, seemed to see the organizational turmoil that was stewing. Besides that, they'd now established a headquarters in California rather than continuing the transient "collective" model. Nope, I was moving on.

DECEMBER 12, 2008

Weston, Connecticut (Super Full Moon)

I'd just hitchhiked from Denver to the east coast in a blur, aiming to see family for Christmas. The last ride I got dropped me off in Chinatown and from there I hopped a subway eager to surprise my old friends at their place in Queens.

I rang every buzzer until a neighbor let me in and I found the door on the top floor open. Sean's girlfriend was startled to see me, but she was conveniently heading to meet him and Mark to catch the train to Connecticut. I had a six-pack of beer ready, perfect to surprise them at Grand Central and tag along to their folks' place for the night.

I always loved surprising friends by just showing up (which only works with certain friends) and catching up on what had happened since the last time.

Somewhat similar to this book I suppose, Mark looked at my visits like little glimpses into my travels thus far. We didn't call or text much, but when I dropped in it was like I had never left, goofing back into our familiar dynamic, just with more stories to tell.

JANUARY 10, 2009

Wakefield, Rhode Island (Super Full Moon)

A holiday party is a good spot to be for the full moon.

I'd met Kayla in Salt Lake City; we were both Couchsurfing with the same host (Candice, who I'll bring up again later). Kayla and I had planned to hitch from Denver to the east coast together, but she'd injured herself snowboarding so couldn't join me.

She was back home in Rhode Island, so I hitchhiked out to see her there, just in time for a nice little party. Her brother turned up with great beer and the lot of us ran around in the snow under the full moon, got a fire going and stayed up until the sun came back around.

The more I rambled around, the more friends I was making and the more directions I was being pulled in. And I hadn't even left North America yet — it's enormous.

I'd later meet U.S. citizens overseas who'd been to dozens of other countries but couldn't point to Utah on a map or tell you anything about the States other than the one they'd grown up in.

For now, I was getting drunk on low-hanging fruit and completely blissed out. Boredom was a far-gone concept.

FEBRUARY 9, 2009

Nashville, Tennessee (Penumbral Lunar Eclipse)

I got hit by a pickup truck, but that's OK.

I'd found a new temporary hitchhiking partner, Woncho, a guy from Couchsurfing on his way to Dallas. Hitchhiking as two guys was noticeably slower than being solo or with a female, but it was still working.

We woke up in Nashville after having couchsurfed with a college kid there, then hitched several rides to Little Rock, Arkansas where we had another host lined up.

Rain and storm clouds blocked any possible view of the lunar eclipse above and while walking into our host's apartment complex I got tagged by the speedy pickup truck.

Woncho ran straight at the driver wielding a miniature baseball bat (he'd stopped at the museum when we passed through Louisville days earlier), ready for confrontation.

Things de-escalated, however, as it was clearly an accident. I slammed my head on the hood pretty good when they braked and bumped me, but nothing was broken; good to go.

MARCH 10, 2009

Lake Powell, Arizona

I started a gasoline fire on Lake Powell. Oops.

Candice, who'd hosted Kayla and me in Salt Lake City, had stayed in touch. I'd seen her a few times, back in Salt Lake and Vegas. Now we'd made plans to travel to South America together and I'd come back to Utah to link up. Spoiler: it would never work out.

She was selling off belongings, we were looking at camper vans online and we were drooling over maps, but it didn't seem like she was fully ready to break away. Either way, I was making more friends over there and going on plenty of mini-adventures in scenic surroundings.

Under this moon, a friend of hers invited us to stay on his houseboat in Lake Powell. We'd found a small sandy beach to anchor near for the night and we'd all gathered some wood to get a little fire going.

Later in the boat, he handed me a lighter and a six-gallon gas jug and asked me to stoke it up. I foolishly swished fuel on the fire, which inflamed the stream back to the jug I was still holding. I reactively tossed it down the beach before catching myself on fire, too.

"You started us a second fire?" they asked when I got back to the boat. Yes, I suppose I did.

APRIL 9, 2009

Las Vegas, Nevada

I got punched in the face at the peak of the full moon.

I'd gotten another free room in Vegas, this time joined by Aaron and his wife Jess down from Sacramento, Walter (from the Alaska collective and hitchhiking with Mandie), and plenty more people we piled in. Between the cases of beers and vodka, the open wine bar we found and free drinks at slot machines, we were pretty saucy.

I drunkenly laid down the last of my known money on the craps table — some 30 or 40 dollars — and lost it all in a hurry. When everyone else called it a night, I took the elevator back down to the casino floor to win my money back by playing poker — a sure thing. Yeah. Sure.

One active table remained at this late hour and I hovered above an empty chair, fumbling through my wallet for a buy-in.

"You don't have enough to play, go home," a player told me.

"You're right," I admitted, holding the only three crinkled dollar bills I could find left. "I barely have enough for a blowjob from your girlfriend."

And so came the punch, and with it security. Then a ban, and then a trespassing charge, and with that, a court date. So I'd be back.

MAY 8, 2009

Phoenix, Arizona

California, Utah, Wyoming, and Colorado. Bikes, booze, digging for marijuana, a Lakers game, and surviving an 18-wheeler molestation — that's all half-moon talk.

By this *full* moon, I was back in Phoenix at Larry's place. Trip Hopping, the travel site I started, was picking up steam and I was coding away, bouncing ideas around with Larry.

I was also staying within range of Vegas, as my court date was less than two weeks away.

When I told security I wasn't going to press charges for getting punched, they then told me I was banned from all MGM properties. I thought that was a bit silly since I was the one who got punched, so I came back just an hour later to try and sneak back into my room.

They caught me, of course. Somehow, wearing a hat didn't disguise the guy with the big camping backpack at six in the morning and this was what brought the trespassing charge.

The date was looming and I didn't know what to expect. All I could do was keep on keeping on, just wait and see.

JUNE 7, 2009

Salt River near Phoenix, Arizona

I destroyed my phone because I thought taking it on the river was a decent idea.

I was back at Larry's having our "Trip Hopping Brew," where we and some volunteers were helping build up the site. This was our version of Couchsurfing's "collective" model.

To take a break from the laptops, we hit the Salt River for a day of tubing. And it was a good day, but my phone was toast. At least it was a productive trip to Phoenix otherwise, though.

A couple of weeks earlier I'd gotten in front of the Las Vegas judge who dismissed my case fairly quickly. Apparently, this trespassing thing happens quite a bit in Las Vegas and they really don't care. In fact, the judge was shocked after seeing my Connecticut driver's license, thinking I'd come all that way from there to turn up to court at all. Happy days.

JULY 7, 2009

Astoria, New York (Micro Full Moon, Penumbral Lunar Eclipse)

The spectacle of competitive hotdog eating drew me back to New York, which is why I was now up on a rooftop party under the moon again.

I'd discovered the annual Nathan's Hot Dogs eating contest just before I started life on the road, which is every Fourth of July in Brooklyn. I hitchhiked from Arizona just to see it again this year and made it in record time: 70 hours from the rim of the Grand Canyon to Manhattan.

Because of this, I stayed with my friends in Queens who held a little party days later that spilled up onto the roof as we raged on.

Maine and Canada seemed like nice places to go next, so they were on my mind next.

AUGUST 5, 2009

Between Hermosillo and Mexico City (Penumbral Lunar Eclipse)

A meth-head truck driver drove us for 24 straight hours.

A girl I'd met in Arizona was looking for a hitchhiking partner and found one in me, blasting down from Canada to meet up with her there.

Thumbing out of Hermosillo, a week into our trip together, we'd caught a ride with a truck driver who was going the distance. We only stopped for fuel and, as I soon found out, meth.

Under the moonlight, parked on the shoulder of the highway, he used a cracked light bulb as his meth pipe, lighting up to keep the ship moving through the night.

By daylight, we were jumping out of his truck at a red light in heavy Mexico City traffic. My new traveling companion was convinced that the trucker had stolen her camera out of her backpack one of the times we'd stopped. We didn't know for sure, but she suspected he'd done so and traded it for meth. Quite possible.

SEPTEMBER 4, 2009

Phoenix to Vegas hitchhiking

Back in Phoenix with Larry for this moon, I was gearing up to hitchhike in the morning to Vegas to meet up with Candice and other Utah friends as a pit stop towards California for another harvest season.

After the meth-head experience in Mexico, that girl and I had also gotten kidnapped, more or less, and spent a night escaping through farmland after bailing out of their truck. We were fine, but she wasn't into hitchhiking anymore, so we parted ways in Merida as I couldn't afford constant bus tickets like she probably could.

But yeah, that's that half-moon talk again; you don't wanna hear about that.

I drank several beers and kicked it with Larry in Phoenix — that's that full moon life.

OCTOBER 3, 2009

Chico, California

Fifty-something marijuana plants stood 10 feet tall in the moonlight and I was responsible for watching out for them.

I was getting paid $100 a night to stay up and make sure no opportunists would decide to hop the fence and rip them off.

All was clear on this night and as the sun came up and the others woke up, it was my time to sleep in the RV. Around midday, I could wake up and make extra money trimming weed, then stay up that night and do it all over again.

Oh, these were the harvest glory days. There was another "guard dog" besides me and we remained friends over the years. I showed him how to homebrew beer, and on that night and most others, we'd kick back some Sierra Nevada beers. Now he works there in the brewery; go figure.

NOVEMBER 2, 2009

Palo Alto to Bakersfield, California hitchhiking

I slept in the bushes by the San Jose airport, fresh off the harvest season.

The idea of going to South America together had faded, but Candice and I were still crossing paths. I'd set her up in Humboldt at another spot I was trimming at, but done with that, we'd spent Halloween at her friend's place south of San Francisco.

I'd left now on my own, but I didn't get very far that day. The bushes near the airport were the closest thing to a hidden spot I could find. Not the best stealth camping, but good enough.

I got pretty good at finding places to tuck away in over the years, even in dense cities. I'd even go as far as to look at a satellite view of the area to find any kind of forest or simply a row of bushes like this.

Waking up, I had Bakersfield on my mind. My first big hitchhiking trip was from Bakersfield to Oklahoma, and I'd couchsurfed with a girl there who I stayed friends with, as well as her dad. Bakersfield itself wasn't much to visit, but I frequently would anyway just to see them.

DECEMBER 2, 2009

New York City

Back on a visit to New York City, I went to my friend's band rehearsal this night. Earlier in the day, I'd gotten cashed up via Western Union for some of the harvest work I'd done out in California, so I was in pretty good shape as far as that goes.

The "green rush" wouldn't last forever. More people were growing weed out there and everywhere, and as laws got laxer, prices per pound would go down too. This, of course, meant growers couldn't afford to pay as much to trimmers.

There were still some good years left, however. Spending a few weeks or over a month working the harvest would often fund my entire year. Since I started traveling, I was living off as little as two grand a year and as much as six or seven.

Being back here in New York was a reminder of how impossible that would have been when I was living there — two grand a *month* was hard to survive on then.

DECEMBER 31, 2009

Connecticut to New York City (Blue Moon, Super Full Moon)

Super Blue Moon for New Year's Eve — that's a good time.

My older brother flew out to Connecticut for the holidays, so I made it there as well. For New Year's Eve, we headed into the chaos of New York City.

My brother had joined the Marine Corps; he'd been in boot camp when the towers went down on 9/11, which is a hell of a time to get started. He'd been all over the world but was now stationed near San Diego where I'd visited him several times along my ramblings.

It was fun hitting the city with him, pinging from one house party to another. I'd made some friends at one rooftop party that mobbed along with me for the duration of the night.

As the sun was just glancing up, we found ourselves passing through Times Square. Hours earlier it had been the center of the media universe, but now it was eerie, empty, silent, as if in a scene in a post-apocalyptic movie.

JANUARY 30, 2010

Mobile, Alabama (Super Full Moon)

At the moon's peak, I was deep in conversation with a girl who'd become one of the bigger "what-ifs" of my traveling life.

I'd spent the day hitchhiking from Tallahassee to Mobile where I had a Couchsurfing host who was also hosting this girl on her way to volunteer on a farm in Georgia — her first outing on the road.

I talked with her all night, even after our host went to sleep, about travel and philosophy and everything we could think of. Back and forth, both curious, both engaged. Her eyes had a dreamy sort of confidence winking through innocence. She'd just caught the wave, and she was riding it.

We agreed that I'd come back east (I was momentarily bound for California) to meet her in Georgia when she was done on the farm. We'd go to the aquarium in Atlanta she raved about and hitchhike together to Texas where she lived.

A fork in the road was coming, and the "what-if" would emerge. And what if there was a second chance? Well, that's coming down the road as well.

FEBRUARY 28, 2010

Carmichael, California (Super Full Moon)

Up at Aaron's, we were homebrewing in his garage amid Sacramento Beer Week.

The "beer week" involved specials all over town. Breweries released different beers, there was a goofy scavenger hunt every day seeking out beer-related milestones, and all sorts of action was going on.

Craft beer had become ingrained in me by this point. When I saw a brewery, I went in. If the person I was staying with showed any interest whatsoever, I convinced them to get a homebrew kit and try it out.

Aaron used to be an unsophisticated animal, and in many ways, he still is. But at least now he wasn't lapping rice beer out of a TV dinner tray or feeling highbrow while drinking Corona out of a shoe. Boilermakers, bowls of loud-mouth soup — you name it with this guy.

No, now he had a little bit of class and I could look him in the eyes when we clinked glasses.

Beer. It's delicious.

MARCH 29, 2010

Eugene, Oregon

I don't think I've ever smoked so much pot in one night.

This was the last night of my first trip with Molly, a girl I'd once couchsurfed with in Flagstaff. It was her friend that I'd hitchhiked with down to Mexico with, and despite how that had turned out, Molly asked me if I'd hitchhike with her to Oregon — she'd never hitched before either.

Our very first ride was from a couple of guys who drove us 12 hours from Flagstaff to San Jose. I told her not to get used to that kind of luck, but it just kept getting better.

On this night, while staying with her friend in Eugene, we smoked from bongs, joints, blunts and everything else. We even had a "box" of beer, something I hadn't seen before or since.

The next morning she'd fly to Phoenix and I'd start hitchhiking south on my own. We'd meet again. And again. And then some more.

APRIL 28, 2010

Flagstaff, Arizona

Terese and I traded kisses under the moonlight to stretch the night just a little further.

I was back to traveling with Molly already; after a couple of music festivals in California, we were on an impromptu road trip with a makeshift crew of wanderers and partiers we'd accrued.

Terese was a friend of Molly's from Flagstaff and we'd hit it off a couple weeks earlier at the music fest, Coachella. Now, after a night of bar hopping, we took a moment alone in the moonlight outside her apartment before climbing up to her room, where the rest of my road-tripping friends had flopped out.

Walter was back in the States backpacking around, about to fly out from Vegas. It didn't take much lobbying to steer the ship that way next, especially given the high chance I'd be able to get a free room.

MAY 27, 2010

Kingman, Arizona

I stared up at the full moon from my bivy tent, tucked behind the only decent-sized bush along the interstate.

Several increasingly ridiculous Vegas trips were behind me, along with memories of camping near Joshua Tree and the rest of the shenanigans with Molly and the rotating crew of characters that joined our whirlwind, one of which she'd eventually marry.

I was back on my own this night, having spent the day hitchhiking toward Mexico. A real estate couple had picked me up and I got lost in their day of surveying properties. I wasn't in any kind of hurry, so joyriding through the remote desert backcountry was just fine with me.

Camped under the stars, my mind wandered to the girl I'd met in Mobile. By the time she was finishing up at the Georgia farm, I was riding the tsunami of energy that Molly and I had stirred up. We hadn't been in constant contact, so when I told her I wouldn't be coming out, I almost thought maybe she'd forgotten about me anyway. She hadn't. A girl after my own heart — sustaining the vibe without the need for constant coercion. She was let down, and I felt it. I was obliterated with abundance and our non-adventure was the casualty of my choice to stay west with Molly.

I'd dwell on it. And still do. Somehow, I'd get a bizarre second chance.

JUNE 26, 2010

Strongsville, Ohio (Penumbral Lunar Eclipse)

By the time the full moon rose in the night sky, I was exhausted from walking and dealing with the police.

I was hitchhiking eastbound and walking on the interstate when a state trooper picked me up, saying it was illegal to walk on the highway, which in this case was true. He dropped me off at the next exit and said I could stand by the on-ramp, but warned me that the local cops might still mess with me. They did, telling me it was illegal to hitchhike, which is not true.

"This isn't the Seventies," the cop told me. Useless. I began walking towards the next town, but before I got to the highway, a cop from that town rolled up on me.

"Someone reported seeing someone with a backpack," was his lame reason for stopping me. So now I had to walk further to the next town, just to avoid any cops who'd already messed with me.

By dark, after 15 miles of walking or so, I collapsed in the woods as mosquitoes feasted on my tired body in the humid Ohio air.

I had interactions with cops here and there while hitchhiking, and even though it's legal, it was usually best not to argue. Play dumb, act happy and best case they leave you alone or even give you a ride. Worst case: days like this one, getting slowed down by ignorance.

JULY 25, 2010

Astoria, New York

In Queens, exercising that audio-engineering degree, I was mixing a six-song EP for my friends. I'd come to town to knock it out as quickly as possible, recording the tracks in their apartment and a nearby studio. By this night, I was onto the mixing phase.

Back when I lived in New York and before the suit and tie job, I interned at a high-end studio in Manhattan run by a guy who used to be the drummer for a big 80s hair band.

At first, I was an intern in the truest sense, answering phones, picking up lunch and that sort of thing. Quite quickly, though, I was helping with studio work and running recording sessions. New projects came in that I took on completely, like adding sound effects to cartoons.

One day my boss handed me an envelope, saying I'd paid my dues and I'd be getting a check like this every week. The check was for $100. For a 50-hour work week. That's all he could afford, he said. Right.

This is what led to the scramble for "any job possible" to pay rent, which became that soulless suit-and-tie job, which ultimately pushed me to the road. I guess it all worked out for the best.

AUGUST 24, 2010

Provo, Utah (Micro Full Moon)

Sometimes it takes a hitchhiker to get you out of jail.

Under the moon, I stood alone at the desolate junction of I-70 and I-15 in Utah. I'd hitched a ride from a guy in Colorado and was tempted to ride with him to his destination in Vegas, but I decided I'd stay on track to Salt Lake City.

When it gets dark, it's hard to be seen and the hitchhiking day is usually over — time to find a place to camp or otherwise. Feeling energetic, I instead planted myself under a streetlight and scored another ride.

A guy listening to a radio show glorifying garlic as the great cure-all was heading to Provo to bail his girlfriend out of jail. He offered to put me up for the night if I'd help him do that in the morning since he didn't have a valid ID to do so himself.

His friends were on meth when we arrived; I briefly sat with them at the table, but then stretched out on the couch and faded to sleep listening to them talk about court dates and the cost of house arrest anklets.

We went out for breakfast and then headed to the jail where my ID was indeed good enough to get his girlfriend out. Happy to help and he even scooted me up to Salt Lake afterward where I was headed to catch up with that whole crew.

SEPTEMBER 23, 2010

Chico, California

Harvest season came back around, and I was awake for the entire full moon night.

I was once again getting paid to guard-dog a marijuana grow. This night, like most nights that month, I'd stay up talking with a friend or working on a project, then pass out when the sun came up. I'd wake up sometime after noon, fertilize or look for pests, and stay up through the night yet again.

I'd first discovered Chico hitchhiking with Walter. He said he couldn't be across the world in California and not visit his friend Donna there. She was a legendary cook and connector of people and good vibes and she instantly became my friend as well. Chico became one of my go-to spots to drop in and catch up with an increasing number of friends or to make a few bucks during harvest.

The town is also home to the Sierra Nevada Brewery, which would surprisingly play a big role in some of my travels moons down the road, a couple of times. Who would guess that drinking beer in California would land you in a paraglider over Nepal?

Oh, beer; you're a beautiful one.

OCTOBER 22, 2010

Willow Creek, California

Still knee-deep in marijuana, but now I'd hitched up to Humboldt County to help out the couple I'd first trimmed for two years earlier.

It would be a lucrative harvest season and I was ready to make moves outside of North America. With every snip of the scissors, I was imagining what was next. Australia was top of mind.

NOVEMBER 21, 2010

Carmichael, California (Blue Moon)

I smoked cigars around the bonfire with Aaron and other friends as harvest season was about wrapped up and cash was in my pocket.

I talked about my thoughts on Australia and luckily more than a few people were telling me that if I was heading all that way, New Zealand couldn't be missed.

I was up for anything.

DECEMBER 21, 2010

New Canaan, Connecticut (Total Lunar Eclipse)

I'd tripped down to Southern California, across the south to Florida and ultimately up to Connecticut for Christmas before leaving the continent.

It was always nice to see friends and family, but I was excited to know that by the next full moon, I'd be in the southern hemisphere, starting what felt like another level of my adventure.

JANUARY 20, 2011

Omamari, New Zealand

Usually, when I see the moonrise or the sunset, that's exactly how it feels — they're rising or falling. Not this time.

With my feet in the sand and my belly full of homemade bourbon, I looked back toward the hilly farmland I'd been lost in hours earlier. Not hopelessly lost, but willingly lost as I followed the sound of the sea. The moon was now emerging above it, as I had, with calm relief.

Turning towards the sea, our orange bowling ball of a star was kissing the horizon, scattering its glow of reflections towards me and the Maoris who'd adopted me for the night — I was the wanderer who came from nowhere to nowhere and was welcomed into their camp.

The sun was not falling. Instead, I felt the massive force of the earth rotating away. I smiled uncontrollably. I sensed my friends and family in the United States past the horizon, gravitating towards the same core of this big, lush rock we were all on. The past three years of memories lit up my thoughts the way a lightning strike looks like a cracked windshield, pulsing and spidering out, then fading into darkness and awe. A faint tear was never able to drop, probably because of the upward pressure of my smile.

One week into New Zealand and I'd experienced so much already. I was in the flow and it was exhilarating.

FEBRUARY 18, 2011

Waiau, New Zealand (Super Full Moon)

The taste of Mauka honey whiskey was still on my lips as I soaked alone in a hot tub; the mountainous countryside faded off and on as clouds floated past the moon.

This was my second night staying with a couple that had picked me up hitchhiking. They were proud of the slice of serenity they'd cultivated on this land and I graciously indulged in some tranquility.

I'd fallen in love with New Zealand, from its natural beauty to the people — like this couple — that had made travel so easy and enriching for the past month.

I'd Couchsurfed here and there, but more frequently, I'd have nights like these, getting invited into people's homes organically. And not just locals — there were nights I'd link up with other travelers. There was a group in a van that picked me up, with whom I camped on the beach; a biking Canadian girl I met while wine tasting who took me to her hotel; and something new every night.

In the summertime bliss, I was just as happy to camp every other night. I'd gotten myself a fishing pole, I'd always had my water filter and along with the stash of food I'd kept I was always ready for a spontaneous hike down the coastline or up a mountain, often going days without seeing another soul. All was good.

MARCH 20, 2011

Queenstown, New Zealand (Super Full Moon)

The Super Full Moon came on a day of relaxation in Queenstown, which was the halfway point of an "adventure tour" I'd lucked into.

While half-moon hitchhiking, I got a ride from a guy who offered to let me stay the night in his spare bedroom. It turned out he was the multi-millionaire owner of a global adventure tour company.

He asked me to help him make a map of New Zealand's hiking trails for his website, and in exchange, he offered me some money, paid the change fee to push my flight back (I was heading to Australia next), and put me on one of his company's two-week adventure tours.

He put me up at his place in the meantime, taking me up in his helicopter a couple of times and even in the two-seater performance plane he had at his own runway down the road. He let me fly it. I did a barrel roll. Over Milford Sound. Wild.

The tour I was on now was with two Canadian couples and the guide, shuttling around the South Island. I'd hiked to glaciers, kayaked, biked around lakes, hiked up mountains, and been eating like a king while spending zero dollars.

APRIL 18, 2011

Sydney, Australia (Super Full Moon)

I spent the day hitchhiking six rides from Mullumbimby back down to Sydney, where I'd flown in a week earlier. I got to the south side of the city and found a place to stealth camp up on a hidden embankment.

Mandie, whom I'd last seen in Vegas, was back home in Australia living in Mullumbimby. I'd popped up to see her first thing and I was now aiming to do a giant loop through the country before visiting her again. Melbourne was my next target.

I intended to use my entire three-month tourist visa in Australia and I was off to a great start. As a kid, kangaroos and boomerangs were more than enough to burn Australia into my brain. The literal "dream come true" was not lost on me now.

MAY 17, 2011

Yeppoon, Australia

I met Bridget directly under the full moon and immediately fell in love, right there on the beach in that moment.

Like the previous moon, I spent the day hitchhiking from Mandie's, only north this time. I'd made that massive loop to Melbourne, up through the outback, northeast to Cairns, and back down to see her. Nick was visiting from the U.S. as well, another friend we'd made at the Alaska collective.

Mandie suggested I stay with her friend Bridget near Rockhampton before bolting west; my next flight was a few weeks away from Perth to Singapore. For whatever reason, I was looking forward to meeting Bridget, even without a face or much of a story to put to the name.

Bridget was fittingly going to a full moon beach meditation group that night and I got dropped off in town just beforehand. Out of a couple dozen souls circled up on the beach, I somehow identified her immediately.

I joined the circle and her hand buzzed in mine as I held it. If you'd told me right then that we'd have a romance that would extend into a rambling travel adventure, I would have believed you. Spot on. That's exactly what would happen.

JUNE 16, 2011

Kuala Lumpur, Malaysia (Total Lunar Eclipse)

Walter (who I also last saw in Vegas) had linked me up with a friend of his to stay with while in Kuala Lumpur.

This was a relaxing moon, coming between sessions of running around the big and busy city to discover its spicy food and high-rise views.

While I was enjoying myself, Singapore and Malaysia were my stepping stones to Thailand, which had me even more excited. That was ahead and behind me was an Australian romance that would be coming back around as well.

JULY 15, 2011

Brussels, Belgium

An epic beer run at a regular old grocery store.

Kasper was someone I'd heard of, been in touch with a bit and was now meeting for the first time in Belgium. He was one of the original coders for the Couchsurfing website, and like myself, he was interested in tech that had to do with our style of travel. If we weren't out exploring the city, we were geeking out at his place on our laptops.

On this particular moon, I'd made an epic beer run to secure some of the classic Belgian brands of beer I'd heard of, as well as some I was seeing for the first time. Chimay, Rochefort, Duvel, St. Bernardus, and all the good stuff. I was amazed that all of this was found in a basic grocery store a block away.

There are many ridiculous stories I could tell from the time I'd just spent in Thailand, but the topic of craft beer wouldn't come up in any of those. I was thirsty now and in the right place.

AUGUST 13, 2011

Istanbul, Turkey

A mosque with big fountains, a colorful spice market and bustling streets all under the moonlight after another day in Istanbul.

I'd hitchhiked there to see Walter, my nomadic friend from the Netherlands who had a travel rhythm of his own. While I'd been go-go-go for the past four years (52 moons now), Walter had been doing the same, except he'd mix it up and occasionally rent a place for several months of productivity somewhere new. He'd then go stir-crazy and get back on that go-go-go until travel fatigue set in and repeat the beat.

This was one of his pauses, one in which he met a Turkish girl he'd ultimately marry and have a child with. He met her hitchhiking into Turkey at the Greek border.

I'd hitched from the rest of Europe to check in on the legend. He was doing just fine, nurturing a tech company he'd started, and obviously enjoying Istanbul and the girl he'd met.

SEPTEMBER 12, 2011

Rotterdam, The Netherlands

Is that Walter in the moonlight again? You bet.

My brother-from-another-mother returned to the Netherlands and after much zig-zagging through Europe, so had I.

I almost lost a shoe while getting waist-deep in the marsh near his house that evening as a group of us walked to the lowest point in the flat country.

Mandie had flown to Europe and was visiting Walter as well. She delivered a bracelet for me from Bridget in Australia; our adventure together was now just a few moons away.

OCTOBER 11, 2011

Yorktown Heights, New York (Micro Full Moon)

Big steaks, New York beers and a late night of catching up with the old man.

I'd just completed my first proper lap around the planet, making it back to New York in time for Sean's wedding. Considering all the traveling I've done, I did a pretty good job of getting to major events and holidays when it mattered most.

I'd known Mark and his brother Sean since the 4th grade. Mark was my age and Sean was my brother's age — a couple grades above us — and we'd been roommates when I lived in New York. I certainly wasn't going to miss Sean's wedding. As far as that sort of commitment goes, Mark wasn't far behind either.

On this night, before the wedding, I took advantage of being in the area to go see my dad, step-mom and little brother. All the rambling and raging was great, but there's not much like kicking back some beers with a belly full of steak and blabbering into the night with your dad.

NOVEMBER 10, 2011

Avondale, Arizona

Having road-tripped west with my Hollywood-bound sister, I was now deep into my travel site project with Larry.

We'd recruited some volunteers for another Trip Hopping "Brew," where the group of us were camped out in Larry's house coding day and night to improve the travel website — and brewing beer to celebrate.

This full moon wasn't all that different from the days that immediately surrounded it. We were percussively pecking at keyboards, staring at screens, flinging around ideas and tipping back a few beers for sanity.

As mundane as that may sound — sitting in front of laptops all day — it was quite exciting and fulfilling. Sites like Couchsurfing were game changers, opening the door for travelers to meet either like-minded or mind-opening people from around the world and do it without spending money on hostels or hotels, therefore extending their trip.

We were expanding upon these hospitality networks as well as making ridesharing and all transportation transparent and accessible.

"Inspiring free and spontaneous travel" was the tagline. It was perfect.

DECEMBER 10, 2011

Chico, California (Total Lunar Eclipse)

Bridget was a lovingly mystical sort of girl, a vegan lover of animals and the spacy little "light dancer" by my side for the foreseeable future. We were kicking back with one of my good friends in Chico during this lunar eclipse.

She'd flown into Los Angeles a couple weeks earlier, in the U.S. for the first time. By now we'd hitchhiked up the Cali coast, camped in the Redwoods and had the entirety of the country between us and our Christmas destination.

She was excited by everything, giggling her way down the road with me. If enough time went by without getting a ride, she'd start doing handstands until it came. The world was our playground.

JANUARY 9, 2012

New Canaan, Connecticut

Bridget and I had hitchhiked clear across the country, having all kinds of adventures only half-moon types would care to hear about. On this full moon, however, I sipped a Dogfish Head Chicory Stout alone after she and my family had gone to bed.

I reflected on the trip with Bridget so far and what was ahead. We had $1 bus tickets heading to Washington D.C. in the morning, only the first of a string of budget bus tickets that would cheat us down to Florida with grand plans to try and hitch a boat ride to South America — or anywhere.

The night was entirely quiet at this hour. My mind was racing but under control. If certain Mayan interpretations were to be believed, then this was it, the last year to dance.

The last sip of beer hit my tongue with intention and I nestled into bed with Bridget. Tomorrow we boogie.

FEBRUARY 7, 2012

Crowley, Louisiana

The moon never shined down on us in a southbound sailboat, despite our musings in the Florida Keys.

Instead, it spotlighted us outside a rural gas station west of Lafayette, which is as far as we got that day hitchhiking from New Orleans. A clerk inside had floated the idea of inviting us in for the night, but after waiting a while for her, we realized she'd left.

We marched down the road in the moonlight in search of a campsite, parsing through the swampy areas until finding a nice hidden (and dry enough) forest area to camp for the night.

Our destination now was undefined, other than the west. Mexico, Peru, California... we weren't settled for sure. The Keys had been full of friendly people; we even wound up sleeping on a catamaran, but no one was going anywhere — The Keys was the destination for them.

New Orleans always delivers, so that had been a solid step after. We both had the spirit and knew the road would show us the way. All we had to do was take the ride.

MARCH 8, 2012

Cabo Pulmo, Baja, Mexico

The Grand Canyon and other little missions came between us and the decision to hitchhike to the bottom of Baja, Mexico.

After some locals showed us how to take advantage of timeshares in Cabo San Lucas for a few days, Bridget and I hitched a ride from a couple guys who took us up the coast, ultimately dropping us off on a desolate stretch of beach as day eased into night.

We basked in the private moonlight, digging into the sand and were in a trance with the sea. We'd reached the bottom and there was nowhere to go but back up, back north, and to the end.

When we crossed into the States, Bridget would only have days left on her visa, so she'd already bought a ticket back to Australia. We hadn't planned our next meeting, whether I'd join her again over there or rendezvous in Europe, Africa, South America, or anywhere.

Lately, I'd become irritated by rudimentary things she might say, do, or not do, and I realized this was more a symptom of missing my solo rambling. There's a certain freedom that's lost when everything is a joint decision or a discussion rather than intuitive action. And so, this night on the beach signaled the start of the homestretch.

APRIL 6, 2012

Vista, California (Super Full Moon)

Bridget has left for Australia, and I'm in jail in California.

Only a week ago, we crossed the border, and within days, she was up in the air. I ping-ponged to Arizona, and upon hitchhiking back toward San Diego to see my brother, I got arrested.

I'd been dropped off near a brewery at sunset, still short of my brother's, so I naturally popped in for a beer to consider my next move for the night. I made friends quickly and before long, a big group invited me to stay for the night, saying they'd drive me up the coast in the morning. Happy days.

A million more beers at their place and all was well but getting hazy. I'd been sent on a mission and the next thing I knew, I was driving the minivan, but as if coming out of a dream, I pulled over to see where the hell I was going. Suddenly, the blue and red lights were flashing behind me.

"You stole this vehicle," is what the cop told me, taking me out of the moonlight and into a jail cell. Confused, my backpack still at my new "friend's" place, I sat through Easter weekend in jail awaiting resolution.

MAY 5, 2012

Chico, California (Super Full Moon)

My friend and I both made valiant efforts to photograph the "supermoon" from her backyard.

Since the last moon, I'd exited jail via a courtroom. I faced two redundant felonies: stealing a car and being in possession of stolen property. That surprised me, as I assumed the second charge was for being drunk as hell. I guess they missed that one.

I was given the option to instead plead guilty to a misdemeanor, the only penalty of which was a fine, which was offset by the long weekend spent sitting in jail — so a wash. The other option was pleading innocence, but that meant coming back, and I wasn't going to repeat that never-ending New York knife dance.

A mysterious week went by before my backpack was retrieved from my "friends" from that night, complete with laptop, passport and everything else I owned. I thought it may have been gone forever, and still, I had no answers. Was the car stolen? Was I gone so long that my "friends" thought I stole it? Why was I even driving it?

Oh well, I had my backpack back, and it would be many moons until I'd figure out how this misdemeanor plea would affect my Canadian travels. Free again in Chico, we laughed at the moon and the beat went on.

JUNE 4, 2012

Bend, Oregon (Super Full Moon, Partial Lunar Eclipse)

After a day of homebrewing, it's nice to hop in the hot tub under the full moon. That's where I found myself this time, in Bend, Oregon, after a jam-packed moon cycle of hitchhiking through the Northwest.

I did see that girl again. The one I'd met in Mobile and planned to hitchhike with from the farm in Georgia to Texas, but then abandoned in favor of the Molly adventures out west. That girl. She was in coastal Washington now, working on another farm.

That story starts with honest confrontation, continues with reinvigorated spirits, becomes flirtatiously light, includes finding a four-leaf clover at a pivotal moment, escalates to passion, and ends with taillights — but all that's under some lame half-moon. I apologize for even bringing it up. Let's get back to Bend, where the beer flows like moonlight.

I'd always heard it was a beer town and that's why I came to investigate. While looking for a host on the Couchsurfing site, I recognized a friend from Salt Lake City and it turned out he'd taken a new job out here as a brewer at a fast-growing spot called 10 Barrel.

With a fridge full of never-ending beer, frequent beer-related events and great new friends, I stayed in town for more than two weeks.

JULY 3, 2012

New York City

I snatched my friend's coworker away from the bar they worked at and galavanted around Manhattan with her, ending with a kiss through closing subway doors before stepping back into the moonlight.

Wild amounts of hitchhiking had landed me in New York in time for Nathan's Hotdog Eating Contest, a Fourth of July staple. The city had never been better. I loved it as a kid, I loved it when I lived there, and as a traveler, it had become even more of a playground.

One night I could be staying with old friends in Queens, the next with a Couchsurfer in Manhattan and the next with someone I met at a bar in Brooklyn. There was no telling who was still living there, who had moved in, or who would be visiting for the week.

The last time I was there was with Bridget, but she and I were no more. Time and distance erode the vulnerable.

Meanwhile, half-mooning through Kentucky on the way to New York, I'd unknowingly met the next girl I'd go on a big hitching adventure with.

AUGUST 1, 2012

Lincoln, Nebraska

"How 'bout some sex?" the big man in the driver's seat asked in a comically high-pitched Southern accent.

"No," I sighed, glad he'd asked before I'd gotten in the car.

"No way?" he tried again, squealing out the window.

I'd hitched out of Indiana the day before, where the girl I'd crossed paths with in Kentucky actually lived. She invited me to spend the night on her couch while I was traveling to Wyoming. It turned out she wanted the same thing this Southern man wanted, so one night on the couch became several in the bed.

No luck for this horny Southerner, however. Minutes later, I was picked up by a guy who not only gave me a ride but also invited me to stay with his family in Lincoln, Nebraska — and wasn't trying to bang.

There had been some awkward propositions like that over the years, but I got pretty good at seeing them coming and shutting them down before they began.

Another full moon of hospitality, with good times ahead and an adventure fermenting back in Indiana.

AUGUST 31, 2012

Snoqualmie Pass, Washington (Blue Moon)

The full moon came on the last night of a 100-mile section of the Pacific Crest Trail with Molly and Kyle. They were hiking the entire 2,650 miles of the PCT together; I just joined for this piece of the adventure.

"Regret" is a hell of a word, one that had come to mind when I'd chosen not to go hitchhiking with that girl from Georgia to Texas. Ultimately, regret wasn't the word to use. Choosing to keep blasting off with Molly had been well worth it. Her, and now Kyle, were friends for life.

We'd met Kyle at one of the music festivals we'd volunteered at. Molly and him hit it off, clearly, as now they were hiking this trail together for months on end.

This section of the trail was absolutely beautiful and no better way to end my short stint with them than camping under the full moon.

SEPTEMBER 29, 2012

Newport Beach, California

I'm on a boat!

While Bridget and I were in the Florida Keys searching for a southbound sailboat, we also posted on some cruising websites. Many moons later, I got a response from a guy looking for help working on an 80-foot sailboat for a few weeks before setting sail around the world. Bridget was out of the picture, but I boogied down to California and was staying aboard with a couple other guys he found on the site.

The owner, Miles, was staying with his girlfriend in Hollywood, but would come down to the boat on most days with supplies and instructions.

Under the sunlight, we built up the inside, scraped rust, painted and did whatever else needed to be done. By moonlight, however, we'd take the dinghy to shore and look for a good time.

This night was no exception, beginning at the cigar shop where we'd made friends with the owner and ending at the beach with the rum bottle we'd manifested. We were drawn to the fire pits like pirate moths, hoping for friendly faces to welcome us into their parties and occasionally we'd take a passenger or two back to the sailboat.

OCTOBER 29, 2012

Newport Beach, California

I spent this day hitchhiking from Northern California back to the harbor. Josh, my crewmate, picked me up on shore in the dinghy under the moonlight. He had beers and stories for me, catching me up on boat life and how things were unfolding. I began getting a more vivid picture of what I'd already been suspecting.

Miles, the owner, had initially told me that we'd set sail in "two or three weeks." It became clear that wasn't the case, which is why I had no problem running up north for a couple of weeks to cash up during harvest season.

Apparently, he was now saying the "earliest" departure would be "sometime in December" and had little to do with the projects we tackled on the boat, and more to do with... Well, he wasn't clear.

I suspected that this boat wasn't going anywhere, not with us, and he was using us as free labor. Cheap labor, I should say. He was supplying us with ramen noodle levels of sustenance.

I fell asleep accepting this reality and I was OK with it. I liked the boat and the shenanigans we'd have on the peninsula most nights, even if we were most likely being fooled. I figured I'd just cut ties before things became boring.

NOVEMBER 28, 2012

Newport Beach, California (Micro Full Moon, Penumbral Lunar Eclipse)

The boat wasn't boring yet. Days in the sun painting, nights running around the beach, cat-and-mouse games with harbor patrol and battles with sea lions kept things interesting.

My brother also lived nearby (a U.S. Marine, he was stationed at Camp Pendleton), and I'd go brew beer with him to get off the boat for a day or two at a time. Also, Michele (the Indiana girl) had flown out for a short stint to stay on the boat with me and trip around that part of California.

On this particular night, Josh and I stopped into one of the only local bars. I caught an odd look from the bouncer.

"Do you remember the other night?" He smirked, knowing that if I did, I probably wouldn't be there. He retold the story of our other shipmate getting kicked out for one thing or another, and how I, siding with my friend, had mooned him from across the street.

I didn't remember all those specifics, but I did remember running to the dingy and my friend falling in the water and pulling his leg into the propeller and the hospital road trip in the sober morning.

DECEMBER 28, 2012

New Canaan, Connecticut

The world hadn't ended, as some Mayan Calendar enthusiasts had hoped. The boat days had gone stale, however, as had the growing list of delays and excuses; it was clear that Miles was using us, but he wouldn't admit it.

I jumped ship and hit the road. Since then, I'd gotten re-banned from half of Vegas again, hitched through Colorado and had all sorts of other adventures the moon didn't shine down upon, eventually winding up in the Northeast for the holidays.

This was a mellow moon, back visiting family and pondering all my options for blasting into a New Year, seeing as I wouldn't be living the pirate life after all.

JANUARY 26, 2013

Albuquerque, New Mexico

I got a late start hitchhiking out of Santa Fe on this day. I'd linked up with Michele in Indiana, hitching east from New York, and again just now in New Mexico where she'd flown in for a nursing conference.

In contrast to the fancy hotel I'd just stayed at with her, after this short day of hitchhiking I found myself camping directly in the moonlight on the west side of Albuquerque on the brink of the desert.

I'd wake up from this, Arizona-bound, thumbing my first ride from a guy who confided in me about a murder he'd committed. The funny thing about hitchhiking is that some people treat you as a stranger they'll never see again and in the intimate confines of one-on-one car conversation, this can become akin to a therapy session.

The short version of this guy's confession is: A guy raped his daughter and he found out about this. The rapist was somehow still hanging around in the inner circle, friendly as can be. So, he (my driver) took the rapist guy on a little trip and made his death look like a drowning accident.

He got away with it and I'm the only person he ever got to tell about it.

FEBRUARY 25, 2013

Surprise, Arizona

Brewing beer and watching a fire show sounds like a pretty good night.

That's what I did, spending it with Molly and Kyle at her parent's place outside of Phoenix. The fire show was all Molly, who'd recently gotten pretty good at fire poi and was showing it off in the backyard.

I'd been hanging with Larry for a bit up until this point, and after this full moon night, my idea was to hitchhike to California. Onward as always.

MARCH 27, 2013

Duchense, Utah

I don't think I slept a wink; we saw this full moon through to daylight.

I'd stopped in to see my buddy Cam in Salt Lake City a day or two earlier to hear the story of his car breaking down on a camping trip outside town. On this full moon, I'd gone out with him and his brother to recover it.

We got to where he'd left the car, along with a tow truck driver, but it was gone. After some calls, we discovered that another private tow truck driver had captured it, or "stolen" it from Cam's perspective.

After a drawn-out confrontation and hesitantly shelling out some cash, we got the car into the hands of the proper tow truck driver, who hauled it back to Salt Lake City.

But, since we were out that way and the guys had all their camping and fishing gear, we made a run for booze and got a fire going at a campsite. We never did camp, though, we were still drinking as the sun came up and smoothly transitioned to fishing in the icy waters.

APRIL 25, 2013

Kingsland, Georgia

Laying in a sweaty bivy sack with a girl I'd met the day before.

It's worth noting that since I began traveling, I have frequently posted stories on HoboLifestyle.com, videos on YouTube and other content around the web.

Rachel, a girl who'd been following me, reached out and asked if I'd hitchhike with her for a stint. She seemed cute and harmless, so I met her in a park in Savannah and we immediately started hitchhiking south together.

Our second night together, on the full moon, and after our first full day of hitchhiking, we were caught just shy of Florida without any light to continue. We stopped at a gas station for a couple cans of beer and started walking until we found a nice hidden patch of woods to tuck into for the night.

The mosquitoes were brutal, and her without a tent of any kind, squeezed into my bivy for a hot and sweaty Georgia night together. Nice to meet ya.

MAY 25, 2013

Bloomington, Indiana (Super Full Moon, Penumbral Lunar Eclipse)

Catfish and beer — another nice moon.

I'd hitchhiked just south of Bloomington to get to a little brewery outside of town and Michele met me there after her day of work for a little feast.

I'd been hanging with her once again in Indiana and this time she said these little visits and path crossings in California and New Mexico weren't enough. She was ready to quit her job or do whatever it took to join me on the road.

My cousin was getting married in Boston and that's the direction I'd be hitching to in the morning. Michele planned to meet me out there and launch off our ramblings together. Despite this inevitability, she cried that night and in the morning like she did every time we split up. It's just as awkward as it sounds, but by now I was used to it.

JUNE 23, 2013

On route to New Mexico (Super Full Moon)

Michele and I rode straight through the moonlit night, hitching a ride in Iowa from a railroad worker heading all the way home to Farmington, New Mexico. The guy was as happy as we were, being that we all took turns driving and sleeping until the sun came up south of Durango, arriving much faster than if he'd been on his own.

Michele was well into the swing of hitchhiking with me by now. She'd met me in New York, gone to the wedding in Boston, then up to Maine, where I got denied at the Canadian border. Remember that California misdemeanor I pleaded to, thinking I was off the hook? Not according to Canada. We banked west instead.

This super full moon ride was the longest we'd gotten together so far. Colorado wasn't even our destination, I'm not sure we had a destination planned at all, but it's where we decided to play around next.

JULY 22, 2013

Hollywood, California (Super Full Moon)

After a stint in Mexico, Michele and I were back in the U.S. and hanging with my sister. We spent the day wandering around Venice Beach and Santa Monica before heading back to her studio apartment in Hollywood.

My sister and I share the same birthday, just eight years apart. She'd moved to Hollywood to go to school for acting and I'd drop in on her whenever I could.

In the morning, we'd be road-tripping up to Wyoming together. Growing up, we'd head there once or twice a year to visit an aunt, uncle and cousins. Shortly after a divorce, our mom had moved out there, too, giving yet another excuse to visit one of the more beautiful patches of the U.S.

Yellowstone, Jackson, the Tetons and all of it. It doesn't get much more beautiful.

AUGUST 20, 2013

San Francisco, California (Blue Moon)

It's Walter again! Any day with Walter is a good day, and he happened to be in San Francisco for a tech conference along with his wife (remember the Turkish girl?).

Michele and I hitched our way over and spent the day with them hitting breweries. I went to some tech lectures with Walter and Michele and I ended the night couchsurfing with another friend I'd met in Berlin a couple years earlier when I'd been hitchhiking to Turkey.

The clock was ticking for Michele, however — we had about 10 days to get her back to Indiana where she had to get back to work. Our idea was to get one last stint of California hitchhiking and bolt back east via the Northern states.

SEPTEMBER 19, 2013

Joplin, Missouri

I slept under the moon next to an 18-wheeler that had picked me up hitchhiking. The driver paused to sleep but was heading all the way to Albuquerque.

I'd gotten Michele back to Indiana and settled her in, witnessing many fits of tears and her depression setting in at the prospect of going back to a stagnant working situation after an electric, free-wheeling summer on the road.

For me, however, it was that time of year again — harvest season. I was bouncing back to California for kicks and cash with the crew out west.

It wouldn't be long until Michele would break ties again. Once you get a taste of the road, staying put seems pretty silly.

OCTOBER 18, 2013

Concow, California (Penumbral Lunar Eclipse)

In the thick of harvest season, I was up the hill a ways outside of Chico, California, where I'd made a good number of friends over my traveling years.

While entering a contest for Sierra Nevada Brewery's "Beer Camp," I met a mutual friend who was growing a whole lot of weed, but also hops along his fence. That's how I wound up in this particular spot.

He wanted to learn how to brew beer, which I showed him, and now I was involved with the main marijuana grow.

I was getting paid to guard-dog, trim, and, on top of that, brew beer for us using the hops he was growing.

Good times.

NOVEMBER 17, 2013

Quincy, California

I'd made a new friend through Couchsurfing in Quincy, which is not all that far from Chico. He'd taken me up in his plane and shown me around town and on this full moon, we'd gone to a jazz show and an afterparty before heading back to his place for the night.

He lived in a big, fun house; I guess it was a mansion, and I had a wing to myself. There was a trampoline in the attic and at one point we even fenced in his library — the type with a wheely ladder that makes you feel wise just by standing in there.

I was one of the winners of the Sierra Nevada Beer Camp contest, along with Aaron in Sacramento, so I wasn't trying to stray too far from California. The Willy Wonka-esque experience awaited us.

DECEMBER 17, 2013

Bloomington, Indiana

Surprise visit!

With Beer Camp in the books, I blasted eastbound. A short, converted school bus picked me up in downtown Sacramento with several people and dogs going the distance — a hell of a ride.

By the full moon, the bus had dropped me off directly in front of Michele's house. She was thrilled. The last time I was there, I'd brewed an Orange Chocolate Stout with her, which she had bottled in the meantime. Under this moon, it was ready to sip on and it was delicious.

She was getting antsy back at work and in one place, particularly with a brutal winter setting in. My presence was just another reminder of the road she'd left.

Instead of watching me hitchhike away the next day, she decided to rent a car and road trip out to the East Coast with me, just to squeeze some kind of trip in. Just fine by me.

JANUARY 15, 2014

Bloomington, Indiana (Micro Full Moon)

Michele drew me back in.

I'd chained a silly amount of dollar bus tickets together to cities between New York, Chicago and finally Indianapolis, with stops and kicks all along the way, dropping in on friends and making new ones.

This day was similar to the others: I entertained myself, Michele would jump me on her lunch break, and when she got off work we'd hang with her friends or check something new out in town.

Bloomington was starting to grow on me. We'd explored all the breweries together and some of her friends were homebrewers, too. So there was no shortage of fun in that department. Like Chico, there was a college town vibe balanced with an overall sense of community. It had farmers' markets, bike baths, a town square and a feeling that everyone you met knew at least one person you knew.

Fun, fun, fun, but the road keeps calling.

FEBRUARY 14, 2014

Lansing, Michigan

Writing stories like these takes some time, and can you imagine if I included all the stories between full moons as well? That's what I was up to in Lansing.

My buddy was leaving town, so I offered to house-sit for him while I delved into laying the groundwork for a book that disregards the moon phases and simply gets into all my stories and travel advice from my years on the road.

Isolation in the dead of a Michigan winter was a great way to start tackling this project — one that's still not done. Or maybe it is? Depends on when you're reading this; perhaps you can give it a search and see if some more moons carved out an opportunity for me to finish.

For now, we have this strobing moonlight of glimpses into the untethered life I've lived, 83 moons deep so far.

MARCH 16, 2014

Boulder, Colorado

Michele is free again!

She quit her job altogether, threw some stuff in storage and we were now hitchhiking together indefinitely. We'd covered a lot of ground since Indiana, down to Memphis and New Orleans, and so on, but on this day we were skiing in Breckenridge.

Michele had a friend who was caring for a big fancy house in Boulder, so we were couchsurfing with her in the "pool house," which was as big as any regular house itself.

Michele didn't have any skiing experience, so she was as nervous as she was excited to get out on the slopes. I was happy to get out there myself and happy to have her by my side again on the road doing whatever made us happy from moment to moment.

APRIL 15, 2014

Near Big Sur, California (Total Lunar Eclipse)

High up and overlooking the Pacific Ocean, Michele and I were camped with about eight bottles of wine that we'd hiked in with.

A day or so earlier, we'd been at a winery (on our way to a brewery) and met a couple that not only took us in for the night, but let us help out at an event at their winery, paying us in wine and putting us up for a couple nights.

We hadn't expected to hike eight steep miles uphill, especially with heavy wine bottles, but that's where we wound up. We'd been dropped off a few miles inland from the Pacific Coast Highway at a campsite after hitchhiking away from our new winery friends. This morning, we saw there was a trail and decided to go for it. It was overgrown with poison oak, steep, and invitingly desolate because of this.

A full moon, alone on top of the world looking out at the ocean, and with a hefty amount of wine: We were in good shape.

MAY 14, 2014

Berkely, California

The fruits of Beer Camp were delivered.

Several moons ago, I mentioned going to Sierra Nevada's Beer Camp, which was a Willy Wonka-like experience. Everything was paid for: big meals, plenty of beer, more beer, scientific beer tastings, tours on steroids — the works.

The culmination of Beer Camp was the opportunity to brew a beer of our choosing (there were 12 campers total in my group). Now that the beer was ready, Sierra was sending each of us campers a keg, as well as sending a couple kegs to a local bar of our choosing for our personal release parties.

Being that I lived on the road, I'd gone to Chico directly to get my keg, and now Michele and I were on a mission of hitchhiking to my fellow campers' towns (most were on the West Coast) to crash their release parties.

Enter this full moon in Berkeley at one such release party. We had many pints of the Ryeway 117 (a rye honey IPA) with Hunter, one fellow camper that we also couchsurfed with for the night.

JUNE 12, 2014

Portland, Oregon

A change-of-pace chill day in Portland, only leaving the house once to hit the grocery store.

We probably needed a mellow day, as Michele and I had been all the way to San Diego and back north in a string of wild hitchhiking days, stealth camping when needed, hitting all the Beer Camp release parties, and forming short road trips with even more beer.

But this night, just mellow, staying at one of Michele's friend's places in Portland, with just one more beer camper to visit up in Bellingham, Washington.

JULY 12, 2014

Teton Village, Wyoming (Super Full Moon)

Michele flew out of Boise to the Midwest for a wedding and I'm kissing some random girl in a mountainside hot tub under the moonlight.

In my defense, not that I need it, Michele and I had established that this kind of thing was fair game when we were away from each other. These sorts of "ground rules" don't have a great track record, not from what I've heard anecdotally over the years, and it probably wouldn't end well for us either.

But if you meet a girl at the bar who knows you're living out of your backpack and hitchhiking to Idaho the next day away from her and her town — and she winds up in the jacuzzi with you anyway? Well, the decision tree on that one is pretty straightforward.

I would indeed start hitchhiking west in the morning with a few stops on my mind, but ultimately to California where Michele would be flying to in less than a week after her trip for the wedding.

AUGUST 10, 2014

Carmichael, California (Super Full Moon)

Michele and I were back to hitchhiking together, but not on this moon. Aaron and his wife wouldn't allow it.

He'd gotten tickets to an A's game and invited me to join him and the crew for a day of beer bars, breweries and baseball. Michele and I were hitchhiking towards Grass Valley for the "North American Hitch Gathering," where several hitchhikers would camp along the river and swap stories for a few days.

We'd gotten a ride going through Sacramento, and I hopped out there, but Michele had to continue and wait for me to catch up a couple days later.

Michele was "no longer welcome" at Aaron's place. The last time I'd brought her over, she'd cried and shouted a few times, feeling endlessly insecure about the relationship. She'd made awkward comments about other things and generally irritated them; they didn't like her and thought I was wasting my time.

The relationship had become shaky, and situations like this weren't positive signs. I'd have other friends and family share the same sentiment, either asking me not to bring her around or just giving me that side eye. For me, she was still fluctuating between tolerable and fun as hell, so I kept at it for now.

SEPTEMBER 8, 2014

Myrtle Beach, South Carolina (Super Full Moon)

Meeting Michele's parents for the second time went far better than the first time.

We crashed in on their prototypical American family vacation in Myrtle Beach. Home of a million mini-golf courses, boardwalks with funnel cakes and gift shops on every corner.

It was a stark contrast to the weeks of hitchhiking it took to get there, sleeping next to highways, seeing friends we hadn't seen in years and rowdy beer nights with random Milwaukee natives who took us in for the night on a whim.

I met her parents for the first time outside of Nashville before we'd hitchhiked together. They were convinced that if I didn't kill their daughter directly, I was certainly leading her to death. After many moons of positive stories, though, they'd apparently turned the corner.

Conversations here were dominated by football, dinner reservations and weather-based wardrobe considerations. But hey, bring a few beers and mini-golf is fun as hell.

OCTOBER 8, 2014

Concow, California (Total Lunar Eclipse)

Up in the hills, I was having the most profitable marijuana harvest season I'd ever had. I was getting paid to guard dog again, paid for the use of my medical prescription (that was a thing for a while) so more plants could be grown and I could make more money every day trimming and tending to the garden.

On this particular night, I was by myself sitting out on the porch when I noticed unexpected headlights parked far down the long driveway that had gotten through the gate. Shit.

The thing about being a "guard dog" is that usually no one actually tries to rob you; simply having your presence known is a deterrent. Now, though, someone was here that shouldn't have been. There were no guns on the property, but I grabbed a club and started making my way down the driveway, not excited about the confrontation.

As I got closer, I got a better look at the "headlights." It was the goddamn full moon being split in half by a single silhouetted tree.

You're lucky, moon. You almost took a beating.

NOVEMBER 6, 2014

Concow, California

A full moon later, I was still up in the hills outside Chico.

At least once a week, I'd head down to town for a night or two to kick it with friends and throw my newfound money at beers and whatever else.

I'd also started regularly hooking up with a pretty local girl who loved craft beer as much as I did. And while this had been a convenient fling, the day after this full moon would bring the return of Michele.

She'd been elsewhere in the country on her own kick, giving me the space to hole up in California for the harvest season. And although we had our "agreement," she'd still ask about this recent girl.

When I told her, I'd forgotten that she'd met this particular girl once before and knew exactly how pretty she was, and so on. The jealous insecurity it caused would never go away. She'd bring up this "threat" even once we'd get a continent away, together, riding side-by-side every hour of every day.

It would be a piece of the downfall, but there were still some decent moons left in us until then.

DECEMBER 6, 2014

Las Vegas, Nevada

Vegas!

Michele and I were staying with the girl I'd met on Couchsurfing when I went to court for trespassing after getting punched in the face. She'd become a good friend by now; I always saw her in Vegas and elsewhere over the years, usually showing up wherever she was bartending to kick off another good time.

We ran around downtown, the moonlight upstaged by the Vegas neon, bouncing between bars and casinos, bumping into friends and finding new ones.

Somewhere in the night, I lost track of Michele as she disappeared to the hotel room to have an impromptu threesome with my friend and her boyfriend. Party on, Michele.

She was among the most sexually starved girls I'd been with. As one example, she told me that while she was in San Francisco, before meeting me at the harvest, she'd let her Couchsurfing host bang her in front of everyone at a voyeuristic bar.

I'm pretty open-minded about all this, but the hypocrisy was not helping her case as she continued to stew over the Chico girl I'd been with. Things were getting testy, even in the party lights of Vegas.

JANUARY 4, 2015

New York City

A year had passed since I'd been in New York, and dynamics had shifted with the moons.

Wives and fiances were emerging; friends had moved apartments, and some had left the city altogether. Even family and friends just outside the city were beginning to fan out around the country. Some might long for the way things were, but I liked watching the evolution in spurts throughout the years.

I'd temporarily shaken Michele in the meantime. She had some obligations and I was content to have some time on my own to catch up with friends and family, which included the misfortune of an uncle who was nearing the end with a brain tumor.

Even though Michele and I had plans of reuniting in just a matter of weeks to go to South America, she'd cried and cried just as she always did when I left. She was loving and affectionate, but embarrassingly submissive. She clung to me, following my lead and rarely suggesting another possible path. When I left, for an hour or a month, it was as if she thought I was gone forever and she'd never see me again.

It sounds like I'm describing a dog, and sometimes it felt that way.

FEBRUARY 3, 2015

Medellín, Colombia

Colombia. I finally made it, and right on the full moon.

Three times before, I'd intended to go to South America, but with Michele by my side, I'd finally broken through.

We'd linked up somewhere in Georgia and gotten ourselves to Florida for the budget flight and here we were staying with a Couchsurfing couple.

We spent the day wandering the city and getting a feel for it and then the night getting to know our hosts some more.

This was the beginning. We had no concrete plan or timeline, but the idea was to keep rambling to the bottom of the continent as we took it all in.

MARCH 5, 2015

Mancora, Peru (Micro Full Moon)

I sat on the side of the road as sunset approached, having just been mugged for all my cash.

I broke up with Michele in Ecuador a week earlier; that day had been inevitable. Days later, I was incapacitated by apparent altitude sickness. I've rarely been sick on the road and that was definitely the most debilitating.

No longer sick, I was hitching on my own toward Lima after several days in a northern beach town. Three guys gave me my fifth or sixth ride of the day, but just a few minutes after picking me up, they were holding me down and taking whatever they wanted.

At the time, I had no bank account, just a PayPal account, but I hadn't been able to renew the expired card before leaving the States. Because of this, I had two thousand dollars in actual cash buried deep in my backpack to last me for the foreseeable future.

These guys dug to the bottom of my bag and found that giant wad, taking that, my phone and a few less important items. Luckily, they spared me my passport, backpack and clothes when they kicked me out of the car at the end of a dirt road in the desert.

APRIL 4, 2015

Yorktown Heights, New York (Partial Lunar Eclipse)

A plane ticket for Berlin had me counting down the days in the New York moonlight.

After things had gotten shaken up in Peru, I journeyed back through Ecuador and Colombia, over to Florida and up the East Coast.

I renewed my PayPal card and had access to money again — the rest of what I'd made in the past harvest. It had been a big year, so although I'd gotten beat for the two grand, I was still in good shape to carry on.

A random search of cheap flights revealed the New York to Berlin ticket, so I scooped it up without much thought as to where and why. And since it was out of New York, I had another excuse to pop in on friends, and on this night, my family north of the city.

MAY 4, 2015

Voorburg, The Netherlands

Walter!

Now married with a little boy and running his own tech company, he still has every ounce of magnetic joy from his backpacking days. I caught him up on my travel stories and he showed me the life he'd been carving out there in the Netherlands.

I was feeling as free as ever. All the time I had with Michele had its perks, but I was remembering now how much more spontaneous and versatile I could be on my own. No discussions about decisions small or large, and no misunderstandings. Just wake up and stay in the stream.

Perhaps there was some balance to be struck that could make a rambling relationship last more indefinitely. Or maybe, that balance was to jump in and out of them.

JUNE 2, 2015

Athlone, Ireland

I hitchhiked to the center of Ireland, to a town called Athlone, only to find that Flannery's Bar was closed on Tuesdays. I'd have to circle back in the coming weeks.

Flannery being my last name, I'd loosely set out to visit every "Flannery"-named bar during my first trip through Ireland. I'd been to several already, starting in Dublin, which incidentally became a story on the radio and in national newspapers. I was a low-key celebrity for a moment.

Since this Flannery's was closed, I hitchhiked back to the west coast and a Flannery's bar in Ballinrobe for some Guinness by the time the moon had come out.

Daylight was fading when I left the bar, but I hitched one last ride from a guy who dropped me off at a shed that belonged to his friend in the countryside. He assured me I could camp there unbothered for the night and he was right.

I felt at home in Ireland.

JULY 2, 2015

Hexham, UK

After hitchhiking down from Edinburgh, Scotland, I camped off the road in the woods west of New Castle.

I was winging it, within winging it, now **100 moons** into winging through my life. Ireland lived up to the hype and more. Scotland showed off its beauty. I didn't know where I was going now, but the UK isn't all that big, so... west it was.

This wasn't my first time in the UK; I'd been there as a kid. After my maternal grandpa died, my grandma took my brother, my cousin and me on a couple of big trips. We'd tripped all over England for a week, and one night we stayed in a castle that had been converted into a hotel.

Langley Castle. This was less than 10 miles from where I was stealth camping that night under the big moon. I sure couldn't afford to stay there, but I dropped in that morning and sweet-talked my way up onto the roof for a little nostalgia.

JULY 31, 2015

Hitching from Nice, France (Blue Moon)

I woke up from a dream of being in the desert with my Uncle Kenny (Butler) on some vague backpacking adventure. It wasn't real. The night before, I'd been on a call with my extended family at my uncle's funeral reception back in the States, taking turns passing the phone to each other.

I missed his life's celebration, but I was at peace. I had his name and I carried his spirit. I wasn't in the desert, but I imagined he was along for the adventure with me.

And good news, uncle: I just fell for a beautiful French girl back in Marseille, and it was time to double back and see what could come of it.

I hitchhiked just short of her city that day, getting from Nice to Toulon to stay a night with some Couchsurfers there. No landscape pairs quite so well with a full moon than a beach and that's where this couple took me that night. Plus cake and beer? We're living Uncle Kenny, we're living!

AUGUST 29, 2015

Oceanside to Los Angeles (Super Full Moon)

Freshly back in the States, I spent this night at my brother's catching up. He was still living near the base, not far from San Diego. Our other childhood friend, Sean, dropped in with his wife too. They'd also move away from New York in favor of the West Coast.

It was Sean's brother and my other good friend, Mark, that had me back in the U.S. — this animal was getting married now, too. The wedding was in New York, but the cheapest Europe-to-U.S. flight I could find was from Denmark to California. That doesn't make a lick of geographical sense to me, but that's how it shook out, so I'd just have to hitchhike the difference back to the East Coast.

SEPTEMBER 27, 2015

**Yorktown Heights, New York (Super Full
Moon, Total Lunar Eclipse)**

Hitchhiking down from upstate New York completed my trip from California, arriving just a few days before Mark's wedding in the city.

It was being called a "super blood moon" that night, and my dad broke out his telescope on the backyard patio. We did our best to photograph the thing, but mostly we were just happy to catch up with some delicious beers in each other's company.

OCTOBER 27, 2015

Memphis, Tennessee (Super Full Moon)

If I've only barely mentioned Nick, it's because he's been hiding from the moonlight until now. We met up in Alaska at the Couchsurfing collective and I've since seen him in more states and countries than anyone else in the world.

Besides the U.S., I've seen him in Australia, Thailand, Turkey, the Netherlands, and so on. He liked to go on year-long round-the-world trips, then dig in somewhere for a year or three, and repeat. Now, he was in Memphis.

I'd hitchhiked from Saint Louis, arriving on the Memphis streets by moonlight and I gave Nick a call. He had no idea I was coming to town because I had no idea either until I wound up there.

A gold-toothed guy approached me with advice while I waited for Nick to come scoop me up. "If you need travel money, you should rob massage parlors. They usually have at least eight grand on hand," were his words of wisdom for me.

About a half hour later I was crushing a dozen donuts with Nick, which seemed way more chill than blowing up a rub-and-tug.

NOVEMBER 25, 2015

Jackson, Wyoming

After getting the wheels turning on a backpack/bivy invention of mine in Georgia, I hitchhiked back west and rendezvoused in Wyoming with siblings also in town visiting my mom for Thanksgiving.

No matter where family had scattered out, I always found a way to check in whenever possible. And Turkey Day is always one of the best times to do so.

DECEMBER 25, 2015

Oceanside, California

A full-moon Christmas — that's a first in my lifetime.

The other half of my family was all here. My dad, stepmom and younger brother all flew out there from New York to my older brother's spot.

Besides catching up with them, I was focused on the crowdfunding I'd started for my "BivyPack" invention. I came up with this idea early on in my travels. It was a hybrid backpack that converted into a bivy sack (a one-person shelter) you could sleep in, using the backpack's frame as tent poles.

It was going well, so I knew I'd have to aim myself toward Augusta, Georgia, where I'd met a guy who'd be helping me with the project.

It would be a choppy year, for sure.

JANUARY 23, 2016

Asheville, North Carolina

Asheville is another town I loved, and this was my last night of a quick visit.

I'd raced across the country, hitchhiking as far as Phoenix, scoring a free rideshare off Craigslist to Tennessee, and hitchhiking the last leg to Asheville. I was Couchsurfing with a brewer I'd met in between South America and Europe the year before. The snow had piled up, enough to shut off the power in town the night before, but either way I'd have to get on the road in the morning.

I had BivyPacks on my mind. The crowdfunding had been a success and I was eager to get to Augusta and get started on production.

FEBRUARY 22, 2016

Grand Island, Florida

I'd gotten to Augusta, Georgia, where James was — the guy helping me make my BivyPacks — but he had to leave town for a bit, which sent me hitchhiking down for a field trip all through Florida.

Hiking, couchsurfing and all sorts of nonsense went down.

I was on the upswing back to Georgia on this night, staying with a Couchsurfing host I'd stayed with a week or two earlier when I'd gotten off the Florida Trail, which I'd hiked a short section of.

I made about $100 that day before dark, doing a bunch of yard work for the woman I would've done for free, but she insisted on paying. A week earlier a guy randomly approached me at a fast food joint asking if I'd help him with some tree-trimming work. Odd jobs a plenty were falling in my lap.

MARCH 23, 2016

New York City (Penumbral Lunar Eclipse)

The crowdfunding money hit my account and materials were ordered when I got back to Augusta, but once again James had to leave town for work. So, once again, I made a field trip detour.

James' work was up in North Carolina, so I rode with him that far and hitched into New York in time for Saint Patrick's Day shenanigans.

On this full moon, I was in Brooklyn, where the now-married Mark had moved to. I was exhausting New York, but having a fun time doing it.

APRIL 22, 2016

Walterboro, South Carolina (Micro Full Moon)

I'm just spiraling around Augusta like a maniac at this point.

Since New York, I'd tripped as far as Memphis and back to Augusta, but after less than a week, James was leaving town for work again. I'd managed to sand some carbon fiber (for the backpack frames), but that was about it.

On this full moon, I was camped near a mosquito-infested swamp, on my way back from South Carolina on another field trip.

James had only left for a week this time and I was ready to get into the swing of making these BivyPacks.

I'd find out the next day that he'd be gone for another couple weeks.

MAY 21, 2016

Biloxi, Mississippi (Blue Moon)

This was the first full moon on my birthday in my lifetime and a blue moon at that.

I'd gotten as far west as San Antonio in my ramblings away from Augusta, but James still wasn't ready to get started.

It was while hitchhiking across Mississippi that I got picked up by Christian, who ended up inviting me to hang out with him and his family. He owned a tattoo shop and he said I was welcome to chill there and get some writing done, as that's what I would have been doing at a random beach town in Florida if I hadn't met him.

"So, when were you planning on telling me it was your birthday?" He asked me midday. I hadn't mentioned it, but I guess he stalked me online and figured it out on his own.

He proceeded to fill me with as much beer and good food as possible. We became good friends and would be seeing a lot more of each other in the moons to come.

JUNE 20, 2016

Augusta, Georgia

BivyPack production has begun!

At last, things were getting moving in Augusta, although I'd soon be going absolutely crazy.

I'd met James a few years earlier when he saw online that I was nearby and invited me to stay the night; he'd been following my blogs and videos for years.

I mentioned my BivyPack idea to him and his girlfriend, who were about to hike the Appalachian Trail. He had experience making hammocks and other gear, and this is how we got started on turning the idea into reality.

On this particular full moon, however, he was once again out of town for work. This time he let me hang back with his girlfriend at the apartment, rather than finding another field trip to go on, so I was feverishly trying to knock this project out.

JULY 19, 2016

Augusta, Georgia

James again left town with his girlfriend for a couple of days on a little trip of their own, but I remained at his apartment, cutting fabric and playing disc golf with his friend Brian.

This was the story up until this point. I'd been doing a lot of tracing patterns and cutting fabric — a tedious but simple task. I didn't know how to sew; that was James' contribution. The only issue was that he wasn't doing much of that. Well, he wasn't doing any of that.

He was home more than these full moons suggest. He, his girlfriend and Brian were a whole lot of fun to hang out with. We played a lot of disc golf, went to an indoor climbing gym and even brewed some beer.

Besides that, I was tracing, cutting, or sleeping. He seemed to have no interest and it was becoming more and more apparent as the days stretched on.

AUGUST 18, 2016

Augusta, Georgia

I'm still here. Damn.

It's now the longest I've been in one place consecutively since leaving New York in 2007. James has completely ignored the project and I taught myself how to sew. There hasn't been any outright confrontation or explanation; it just slowly became the way it was, with me doing everything, that is.

Once, when he was out of town, his girlfriend confided in me that she wasn't sure why he wasn't helping either. She said it had never been brought up and she didn't want to be the one who did. It was all a bit bizarre and somehow past the point of confrontation.

I was frantically trying to finish making all these BivyPacks for the 30-plus people who'd been waiting since January. I was sprinting to finish before things got any more awkward in the apartment and before I reached absolute insanity.

I needed the road. This full moon night might as well have been any other night that month and that's not great. At least I'd bought the mailers a day before; that was new — I was getting close.

SEPTEMBER 16, 2016

Interstate 40 in New Mexico

Freedom!

I went directly from the post office to the highway the day it was all over in Augusta. BivyPacks are in the mail and I'm back on the road.

While this moon is in the sky, I'm in an 18-wheeler heading for Arizona. He'd picked me up hitchhiking out of Indianapolis and told me he was going all the way to Scottsdale.

I was ultimately heading to Molly and Kyle's wedding in California, so this multiday ride was a hell of a score. The driver even loaded me up with truck stop buffets along the 1,700-mile trip.

Gotta love looking out at that full moon from up in a big rig.

OCTOBER 15, 2016

Chico, California (Super Full Moon)

A makeout session on a porch in the moonlight is always a win.

I was in Chico trimming again and right in town this time. So compared to being up the hill, there were a lot more nights out at beer bars and house parties — all pretty good times when you're getting cashed up every day.

On this particular night, there was a party at a makerspace. I'd met a girl that night and things had spilled back to one of my friends' places.

Oh, Chico. You always deliver.

NOVEMBER 14, 2016

Carmichael, California (Super Full Moon)

Taking a break from Chico, I dropped in to see Aaron and company. That crazy bastard.

I'd just won another contest with Sierra Nevada, so I was pondering my next big move. Not Beer Camp this time; instead, it was an "adventure photo" contest, which rewarded me with a choice of adventure trip options around the world.

Kiteboarding in Costa Rica, climbing mountains in Africa, taking a boat ride to the Galapagos — my wheels were spinning. Aaron's garage was a good place to ponder such things, even if he was an absolute animal.

DECEMBER 13, 2016

Reno, Nevada (Super Full Moon)

While hitchhiking east, I got a ride from a girl who was convinced that her next diet would be oxygen-only. No water, no food; just breathe it in. All natural.

She dropped me off in Reno under the moon and I never saw her again. I'm not sure anyone has.

Anyhow, I found myself a room at a casino to pause for a day or two. My little brother and sister were flying to our mom's in Wyoming for Christmas, so I made that my destination as well, knowing I'd soon be skipping off the continent again.

JANUARY 12, 2017

Phoenix, Arizona

I'd chosen my trip after winning the Sierra Nevada contest: a two-week adventure tour through Nepal.

Sierra had additionally given me a staggering $3,500 in order to take care of the plane tickets and other expenses. That's about what I've been living on per year since I've been on the road, so I was about to stretch the hell out of it by taking the long way to Nepal.

My first plane ticket was already paid for: Las Vegas to Honolulu. I'd been to the other 49 states, so I figured I might as well check out the 50th on my way to Asia.

This was my last moon in the continental U.S. for a while, so I was hanging with Larry in Phoenix before getting to Vegas for the flight. I'd ordered some fabric and was making a new prototype BivyPack for myself, too, now that I was a sewing expert. It's a lot more chill making one, instead of 30-plus, that's for sure.

FEBRUARY 10, 2017

Waikoloa Village, Hawaii

Every day in Hawaii was a new adventure. By this moon, I'd made it from Oahu to the Big Island. After doing a lap hitchhiking along the coast, I doubled back to Waipi'o Valley.

I hitched a ride down the steep road to the beach at dusk; there were some people on the beach, and I wanted to get out of the way. I knew of a foot trail that went further to Waimanu Valley, which I was told was even more beautiful and remote.

I wasn't going to hike the eight or so miles in the dark, so I walked down the beach away from people. I crossed a stream above my waist in the moonlight; it flowed from the woods to the ocean.

I found a place to tuck away, hidden, although several wild horses walked by me throughout the night.

MARCH 13, 2017

Durack, Northwest Territory, Australia

My last day in Australia was spent with a Couchsurfing host and two Germans who were also traveling around Darwin. We went to a series of waterfalls that day, one accented by a rainbow, then headed back to town facing a beautiful sunset.

I'd seen Mandie earlier on the East Coast, of course, and she talked me into starting my podcast, the Freestyle Travel Show. I even saw Bridget briefly for the first time; it had been 61 moons since hitchhiking together in North America. Mandie and I visited her at a house she was looking after. She looked beautiful.

In the morning, I'd be flying up to Bali for my first run through Indonesia, inching my way to the adventure in Nepal.

APRIL 11, 2017

Oudongk, Cambodia

Puttering down the dark road on the back of a motorbike, I had no idea where we were going and didn't share a common language to figure it out.

I'd hitchhiked out of a beach town that morning, Preah Sihanouk, where I'd swam in bioluminescent waters while making temporary friends at a hostel.

I was barreling towards Thailand now, except, on the back of this bike, maybe not. We were definitely going in the right direction when he first picked me up. We'd stopped at one point, where I imagined he was turning, and I attempted to indicate that I was going to find a place to camp for the night and thanked him for the lift.

Instead, he motioned for me to get back on the bike. He took me to two different hotels, both of which were either full or cost too much money. Again, he motioned for me to get back on the bike, but this time we rode for an hour in an unfamiliar direction.

We arrived at a shack, his home, where I met his friendly family and ate a bowl of soup (that I'd vomit up a day later). I slept under a mosquito net and walked out in the morning, getting my bearings and pointing back toward Thailand.

MAY 11, 2017

Kathmandu, Nepal

Jane and I lounged out in the 18-wheeler truck we'd hitched a ride with, heading back to Kathmandu. The next day I was heading to India.

The "adventure trip" I'd won from Sierra Nevada was actually a trip for two, which makes the amount of money they gave me for plane tickets make more sense. Try as I might, I hadn't been able to find anyone willing and able to join me on the adventure.

That was until just one day before. Not wanting to waste the free pass, I posted on a Couchsurfing message board, being extremely vague, asking if anyone wanted to link up for a "mystery trip" for a couple of weeks. Jane is the only person who responded.

Jane was from the UK and had been backpacking around the world for about a year. When I got her on the phone, she was at the airport in San Francisco with a ticket to Kathmandu. When I explained the trip (whitewater rafting, paragliding, elephants, hotels and meals paid for, etc), she was ecstatic.

She was accustomed to hitchhiking, camping and couchsurfing like myself, so we both lived high on the hog for the two weeks. Now that it was over, we were back to our hitchhiking ways, bound for Kathmandu where we'd part ways.

JUNE 9, 2017

Serres, Greece (Micro Full Moon)

Molly and Kyle!

A bunch of doctors and medical folks from the UK had picked me up hitchhiking the night before in Bulgaria for a music festival and they'd put me up in their AirBnB in Plovdiv after partying all night.

I hitched 15 rides to get to Greece, which is a lot for one day. I think my record is 25 or thereabouts, but 15 is plenty. I'd gotten dropped off in Melnik, a quirky little town that I almost camped near, but instead got some wine and mousaka and kept it moving.

I got dropped off at the border with Greece and somehow walked across it undetected. I had to walk back for them to stamp my passport, which had border patrol and police pointing fingers and blaming each other for letting me slip through like that.

One more ride and I got close enough to Serres for Molly and Kyle to pick me up. They were helping refugees there and had just returned from hiking the Jordan Trail — I believe they were among the first to hike the trail in that country.

India and Dubai behind me and all of Europe ahead, I was happy to catch up with great friends before journeying on.

JULY 9, 2017

Kosice, Slovakia

One of the greater benders of my time started in Budapest a few days earlier and this moon was the midpoint.

I'd met Bob at a bar there back in Budapest. After drinking and talking, it came out that he had tracked his ancestral origins to a small town in Slovakia. He didn't know anyone there; he didn't have any leads, but he wanted to go and he asked if I'd join him.

He insisted that he'd cover buses and rooms after I'd brought up hitchhiking, not something he was interested in. And so began the bender — a never-ending stream of beers, shots, whiskey Cokes and everything else from sun up to sun down as we traversed cities, ganging up with other travelers for hours or days at a time.

This full moon was spent in the city of Kosice, where he'd rented an Air BnB. We'd attracted several Couchsurfers who hit the town and flopped out in the apartment as well.

In the morning, we grabbed Irish coffees and wine for the bus ride to Medzev. The drive was absolutely beautiful, followed by slums, and finally, the picturesque town of his ancestors.

After much drinking and giving up, we actually did stumble into someone with his last name. Go figure. Off to Poland to keep the party going.

AUGUST 7, 2017
Porto, Portugal (Penumbral Lunar Eclipse)

"Hitch Fest" was a gathering of hitchhikers in Portugal, where I was asked to give a workshop. Pretty casual but lots of fun, with around 100 hitchhikers camping out for several days, sharing stories and jamming to music.

I hitchhiked there with Oceane, a beautifully named girl I'd hit it off with a couple years earlier in France. We'd gone to the "Hitch Gathering" then, which was more informal but has been a long-running annual meeting point for hitchhikers in a different part of Europe each year. I went to the North American gathering with Michele years earlier, which always had a much smaller turnout compared to Europe.

Hitch Fest was over by this moon, but Oceane and I remained in Porto, exploring the town and stealth camping on the outskirts. If it had been up to me, I would have weaved through the planet indefinitely with her.

As I've learned, though, travel love is delicate. Two fickle minds race along, trying to find a balance between too much time together and too much time apart, trying to stay in sync and dance along without discovering stagnancy in each other or being drawn away to another shining light. It's a rare kind of magic.

SEPTEMBER 6, 2017

Athlone, Ireland

We end our decade of moons together at Flannery's Bar in Athlone.

This was the Flannery's I had to circle back to on my first trip to Ireland, which appropriately made it the finale then as well. Anne Flannery runs the place, and while I have no proof, I have to imagine this fun-loving soul is my blood.

The local newspaper had come to take photos, my Couchsurfing host and her friends were game, and we'd stayed until the sun came up. I even had to get in front of TV cameras, as they wanted to cap off my little adventure visiting Flannery's bars around the country.

This time around, I stayed with the same people and the times were just as electric. The Guinness and whiskey flowed as another night on the never-ending road roared along.

Ten years, 127 moons and no signs of slowing down. Hell, that's just the first decade of moonlight; let's keep dancing.

About The Author

Kenny Flannery left his apartment in New York City in the summer of 2007 and has been living out of his backpack ever since. You know this by now.

He hosts the "Freestyle Travel Show," which you can listen to anywhere that podcasts are found.

Stories and advice from the road are also shared regularly at https://www.hobolifestyle.com and he has written another book called "A Six-Pack of Hitchhiking Stories."

Exclusive content is available to those who want to further support his travels: https://www.patreon.com/kennyflannery

@HoboLifestyle everywhere else, like YouTube and the socials.

Printed in Great Britain
by Amazon

20769367R00079